Getting the Buggers to Learn

DUNCAN GREY

continuum

Continuum International Publishing Group

The Tower Building   80 Maiden Lane
11 York Road   Suite 704
London SE1 7NX   New York
                             NY 10038

www.continuumbooks.com

British Library Cataloguing-in-Publication Data
A catalogue record for this book is available from the British Library.

ISBN: 0–8264–7835–2 (paperback)

Library of Congress Cataloging-in-Publication Data
A catalog record for this book is available from the Library of Congress.

Typeset by BookEns Ltd, Royston, Hertfordshire.
Printed and bound in Great Britain by
Antony Rowe Ltd, Chippenham, Wiltshire.

Contents

Introduction

Do we show our pupils how to learn? Or do we expect them to learn by osmosis? If they don't want to learn now, we can at least give them some tools to use if they want to learn in the future.

This book is about learning to learn. It looks at information literacy strategies, learning styles, study skills and thinking skills. The strategies of learning to learn can be carried out in every lesson, every out-of-school activity, tutorial times and assemblies. They work best when embedded naturally in daily lessons. Learning to learn is a skill for all learners at all times. Learning to learn is a skill for life so our pupils will be able to cope and adapt in an ever-changing learning world. As Charles Leadbeater (2005) has said: 'The frontline of learning is not the classroom but the bedroom and the living-room'.

How do you teach?

Do you have a narrow range of techniques that work or do you aim for variety? On a piece of paper, answer the following questions based on your own current teaching and on your recent observation of other teachers' lessons. You could also ask your pupils what they think.

Which three of the following teaching techniques do you and your colleagues use most often in class?

Students ...	Your class	Colleagues' classes
Copy from the board or a book	☐	☐
Listen to the teacher talking for a long time	☐	☐
Have a class discussion	☐	☐
Spend time thinking quietly on their own	☐	☐
Work in small groups to solve a problem	☐	☐
Take notes while the teacher talks	☐	☐
Talk about their work with a teacher	☐	☐
Learn about things that relate to the real world	☐	☐
Work on a computer	☐	☐

When you've recorded your results, compare your answers with the results of a *MORI survey* taken in 2000 and 2002 (see p. 216 of this book). How do you compare?

All of these can be learning activities and all, if used to excess, may hinder rather than help learning. What do you think?

- What is your reaction to the pupils' answers in the MORI survey?
- Are you surprised, shocked or do you approve of the frequency?
- Do you approve of the change in frequency over two years?
- Many people would say that the changes in those two years go against the perceived change from traditional 'chalk, talk, sit, listen' to the 'discuss, negotiate, work in groups' approach. Do you agree?
- Is this because the perception was always wrong, or is it a reaction to the cries of traditionalists?
- Do the results give any suggestion that the proposed learning future of solo, online, task driven, computer-mediated, distance learning is on its way?
- Which of these activities will best help our pupils to cope by themselves with future change?

If you had to present these findings at a staff meeting, which of the nine activities above would convey your message most effectively? Which of the nine would you personally be most comfortable doing?

Think of the way you prefer to do things. Do you prefer to

- talk face to face
- phone someone
- email them
- hand-write a letter?

When you use a computer how do you interact with it? Do you prefer

- a keyboard and keystrokes
- a mouse and menus
- a joystick
- touch-screen
- speech technology?

If trying out software for the first time, do you

- read the printed manual
- read the online manual
- watch an introductory video
- ask someone for personal help
- just click and hope for the best?

When you need to communicate by computer with other people, do you prefer to

- attach a Word document
- send an email
- join a threaded discussion
- take part in online chat?

When you view web pages, do you prefer to

- move quickly between many screens
- scroll down a few longer screens?

What kind of web pages do you prefer?

- mainly text
- mainly graphics
- animation
- interactivity

Our answers will probably differ from those of our pupils. My pupils have different preferences to mine and we are both different from my 80-year old father.

Attention spans, motivation and purpose will affect the way we want to learn and our age and experience may mean an interface designed for a 12 year old is incomprehensible to a 70 year old.

So, while computer-based learning may seem to be an asocial activity for geeks and loners, some computer users love the way they can chat and correspond with online buddies or work cooperatively with other users. While physical learning and computers may seem to be a contradiction, some learners are attracted to the interactivity of software games which show processes and activities. Linguistic learners will prefer text-based pages and the ability to manipulate words in a word processor or bring them to life in animations, while visual learners will go for graphics software and graphically rich pages.

The identification of Intrapersonal, Interpersonal, Physical, Linguistic and Visual learners can be a good way to make sure that the learning experience is richer for all our pupils.

While modern computer software can provide for the needs of different learners and can encourage learners to adopt a wide range of learning styles, traditional methods are no less important than computer-based experiences. The emphasis should and can be on variety and choice.

There is more about learning styles in Chapter 4, but looking at preferred learning styles – our own and those of our pupils – is as good a way as any to introduce the topic of learning.

The big question is, how do we introduce effective learning into a modern curriculum crammed with attainment targets and a classroom crammed with restless children?

According to the Hay, McBer Report (2000), effective teaching is characterized by:

- all pupils being actively engaged and involved in the lesson
- the lesson being linked to previous learning or teaching
- the ideas and experiences of pupils being drawn upon
- clear instructions and explanations being provided
- a high level of interaction between the teacher and the pupils
- the teacher being able to listen and respond to the pupils
- questioning being used to consolidate, extend and probe pupils' knowledge and understanding
- a variety of activities, each of which has a clear purpose and is appropriate to the stated learning objectives.

What we teach today in terms of content will probably be outdated within a decade and certainly before the working lives of our pupils are halfway through. However, what they learn in terms of attitude and basic principles should last them a lifetime.

Our pupils must learn how to learn, because they will need to learn and relearn, often several times, in their lives.

Give a child an answer and you satisfy him for a moment.
Show him how to learn and you satisfy him for a lifetime.

And in case you think that's all a bit airy-fairy, believe me when I say I have taught these skills to resentful adolescents who couldn't at first see the point of it all. Some criticized me for not immediately answering their short-term questions; some accused me of doing nothing because I deliberately took a back seat while they worked on my patiently crafted learning materials. Some, however, realized that this was a kind of independence, which elsewhere in their lives they were struggling to achieve.

Where we came from

There are three reasons why we need to look again at our teaching and learning styles:

1. Pedagogy – the way teaching and learning has changed
2. Information and the amount of it there is all around us
3. Skills and the need for them to make the most of the information

The way we teach

We have moved, in just one generation, from a traditional 'chalk, talk, sit, listen' approach to a discussion, negotiate and work in groups approach, and we are approaching a solo online task-driven, distance-learning approach. Is it working? Should we have a range of approaches rather than one that is fashionable and new? Have we got the balance right?

Chalk, talk and listen

The traditional 'chalk, talk, sit, listen' approach is exemplified by this extract from Dickens' *Hard Times*:

> *'Now, what I want is Facts. Teach these boys and girls nothing but Facts. Facts alone are wanted in life. Plant nothing else and root our everything else.'*
>
> *Cecilia Jupe (who works with her father in the circus, with horses) – your father is '. . . a veterinary surgeon, a farrier, and horse breaker. Give me your definition of a horse.'*
>
> *(Sissy Jupe thrown into the greatest alarm by this demand.)*
>
> *'Girl number twenty possessed of no facts, in reference to one of*

> *the commonest of animals! Some boy's definition of a horse. Bitzer, yours.'*
>
> *'Quadruped. Gramnivorous. Forty teeth, namely, twenty-four grinders, four eye-teeth and twelve incisive. Sheds coat in the spring; in marshy countries sheds hoofs, too. Hoofs hard, but requiring to be shod with iron. Age known by marks in mouth.'*
>
> *Thus (and much more) Bitzer.*
>
> *'Now girl number twenty,' said Mr Gradgrind. 'You know what a horse is.'*

Nevertheless, this teaching style has its advantages. The teacher is readily identified, so the focus is on dissemination of information by a single person. By his own personality the class, usually sitting and listening, can be given instructions or information in an efficient way. Discipline is maintained by the eagle eye, and conformity is encouraged. This is 'filling up the little pitchers with knowledge'. When the teacher is respected the atmosphere is orderly and has the potential for an effective learning environment. This style is economical on a teacher's energy because it is controlled and predictable.

Few of us would prefer the harshness of Gradgrind to the sensitivity of poor Sissy. Yet the barrage of assessment targets, constant testing and examinations is more likely to produce a boy like Bitzer than a natural learner like Sissy Jupe, who knows more about horses than Bitzer ever will, but can't formulate her knowledge in rigid academic terms.

And for those who think of Gradgrind as belonging entirely to Dickens' fiction, I remember at the end of my first year of teaching asking a senior colleague what he thought of the 'old-fashioned view' that a teacher should never smile before Easter. He turned to me balefully and hissed, 'Why bother then?'

However, while the teaching may be efficient, how much learning takes place, and what kind of learning is it? Some information will certainly be absorbed and a well-organized lecture can transfer information from one head to thirty (or hundreds) others. Note-taking can help retain some of this information. However, lasting understanding and empathy is limited.

> I hear and I forget
> I see and I remember
> I do and I understand

Chalk, talk, sit and listen, while remaining a very common way of teaching, is stuck in the forgettable category, which – for many of our pupils, especially the less able – makes it a second-rate way of learning.

Discuss, negotiate

In the popular current 'discuss, negotiate, work in groups' approach, the emphasis is moving from teaching to learning. There is, of course, a risk that learning disintegrates as teaching becomes less dominating.

In this approach, a pupil's behaviour could be more challenging because the teacher's presence does not dominate. On the other hand, it may be more reasonable and sociable because pupils are more actively involved and engaged. There is not the large audience of a full class to play up to, or an authority figure to challenge.

Discussion is an excellent way to test a child's opinions against others. The reactions of fellow pupils can be decisive in forming our opinions. What to some may seem like idle chatter can be purposeful interaction, though the role of the teacher in maintaining on-task activity remains important.

In the picture above it is hard to work out who is teacher and who is the pupil. The formal classroom itself and the hierarchy that goes with it have disappeared but the focus on learning is clear.

In this kind of cooperative learning, formal assessment usually remains necessary to separate the individual's input from the group activity. Yet the greatest learning of all may be taking place in the personal acts of negotiation and cooperation within a small group. Continuous coursework and sudden-death examinations do co-exist under the present system, yet each tests only a limited range of skills and knowledge.

There is an emphasis on understanding rather than memorizing and, while some rote learning takes place, it is supported by learning by doing. As pupils are asked what they would do in this or that situation they are encouraged to imagine how it would feel to be there.

This style of teaching means the teacher is not always at the front of the class, but at the side, watching, intervening from time to time, to guide, direct and to provide learning opportunities.

Solo, online, distance or e-learning

The future holds the prospect of solo, online, task-driven, distance learning, learning for life, e-learning. If our traditional model is teacher on a dais at the front and the more liberal view is of teacher helping from the side, here the teacher seems to retreat to the back of the class – or even into the distance! Indeed in many computer room layouts pupils literally have their backs to the teacher.

The emphasis must turn towards *learning how to learn*, where the learner is responsible for his or her own learning and can choose from a range of modules and courses. This kind of flexible learning offers variety and real differentiation and involves coherent management by teachers. The learner needs to be self-motivated for it to be successful, though the alternatives on offer do offer something for everyone. For the teacher, the immediate task is supporting the higher educational vision of helping pupils to learn for themselves.

Although it is unlikely – and unhealthy – that all, or even most, school-based learning will take place via a computer, the advantages of freely available extensive communication, information sources, editing, collaborative and presentation tools suggest that the 'wired classroom' and computer-mediated learning activities will be with us for some time. For post-school training it may often be the only practical solution.

So, what becomes of the teacher? Are we still relevant in this brave new world? Do we become disciplinarians or, even worse, professional motivators? It seems more likely to me that we will have to work in cooperation with others, who, given the amount of money available, would probably be 'para-professionals'.

Technical support will be needed and training in these new methods is essential for educators and learners alike.

Librarians and learning specialists must be at the centre of this development. A new breed of educationists with a background in learning theory, materials production, information technology and information skills will be needed to produce learning materials of high quality. Hand-written photocopies and Banda sheets are no longer enough!

Information professionals (we used to call them librarians!) may be connected to schools. Many institutions now have learning-technology professionals within their support services and some offer e-learning masters' programmes.

Learning technologists are becoming recognized as an important breed of new professionals providing a valuable institutional role spanning the technical and educational aspects of using technologies for learning.

However, there is still a dearth of these professionals in senior roles or at government and policy level and there is not yet professional recognition for these roles.

Our roles are changing. How do we cope?

Schools and teachers must adapt to changes in learning. How can we help pupils to cope with future learning needs? How can we help them to make the right choices?

As Hogwarts Headmaster Albus Dumbledore says to Harry Potter: 'It's our choices, Harry, that show what we truly are, far more than our abilities.'

Learning is not just cramming in information, 'filling the little pitchers with knowledge' as Gradgrind has it. Firstly, there is essential interpreting and understanding of that information, then applying the knowledge which that information brings. In other words it's not just what you know, it's what you do with it.

Then, above and beyond the information itself is the understanding of how to learn more. It's not enough to be content with what you know now, you have to know how to acquire knowledge for the future. By definition, tomorrow's knowledge doesn't yet exist and has still to be learned. We can teach fundamental principles and current knowledge but we must also teach the skills of learning to learn, of tapping huge information sources, selecting what is useful and using it to solve problems.

As teachers we have a duty to help our pupils to learn for themselves and become independent.

Pupils

Virtually all of today's school population have had frequent ICT training and practice throughout their school lives and most have developed useful skills. They expect mobile computing and communications at home and at school. But while they may be familiar with word-processor menus, paint programs and entering a word into a search box, they are often less familiar with repurposing text, selecting and filtering search results and coping with the vast amount of information there is available.

Some will show off their knowledge to us in an attempt to show their superiority. However, the highest skills are not how to animate text or insert a new column in a table, but how software can enhance learning and how we apply knowledge to new situations.

It's a salutary lesson to come up with a fancy new worksheet, all colours and clip art, then to be asked, 'And what are you going to *do* with it?'

Students

Many now have access to a PC at home and most of the expected 50 per cent of pupils who go on to further or higher education will use Internet connections in their student accommodation. Today's school leavers have had IT training and practice throughout their school lives and most have developed useful skills. They expect mobile computing and communications.

However, many are not skilled in filtering and interpreting the large body of information to which they have access. They urgently need learning skills and information skills. Independent for the first time they often struggle without a teacher at hand.

Just as from time to time they need advice in managing their bank account or how to cook a chicken, many sixth-form or university students are not yet independent learners.

Teachers

Large numbers of teachers make use of email and the Internet to support teaching and research. We may not need to develop our computing skills to the point where we can teach a computing course but we may find it helpful to develop more sophisticated use of e-learning strategies to support our teaching.

We need to be aware of the support we can receive from other professionals and be able to define our needs in sufficient detail so that technicians and programmers can match our needs to software, hardware and specific materials.

We should also be familiar with presentation methods and software we can recommend our pupils to use.

Librarians

School librarians have a unique overview of learning-resource needs across the curriculum. They have this map in their heads already. They are accustomed to conducting intelligent searches, organizing and cataloguing a wide range of resources.

Generally their ICT skills are at least as good as teachers', with a particular emphasis on search engines and keywords which they adopted at an early stage. For many, the school library has been changed from a humble collection of books to a virtual library encompassing electronic data from all over the world in a variety of media. In school the librarians are gatekeepers for the world's learning resources.

We need to develop a closer liaison with these fellow professionals in the development and delivery of courses and learning materials.

Course designers

Course designers are usually teams with skills in graphic design, programming, learning theory, writing and editing. They know how to attract the learner and induce learning by presenting attractive and interesting interactivity. They know it is not enough to tell – what's needed is involvement and interaction which will stimulate thinking.

Learning technologists

From course designers will come the relatively new role of learning technologist – combining many of the skills of the course designer team. 'Instructional Technology is the theory and practice of design, development, utilization, management, and evaluation of processes and resources for learning' (Seels and Richey 1994).

More simply, it is any application of technology, particularly computer and information technology, which contributes to the learning process. With pupils increasingly expecting their school-based learning materials to match professional commercial products, it is no longer reasonable to expect classroom teachers to produce commercial quality resources in their preparation time.

A learning technologist will be familiar with existing 'learning objects' which can be combined into new sequences to create individualized learning experiences, and will have the skills to write additional learning objects for specific needs. These may include simulations, interactive models and virtual tours.

Senior managers

Senior managers in schools have been slow to understand the strategic issues generated by e-learning. Many still think in terms of providing more and more powerful computers rather than establishing how blended learning can best take place, combining face-to-face with computer-mediated learning.

Parents

Parents will increasingly appreciate that learning takes place informally at all times and that there are learning opportunities which don't involve formal training. They will have to make their own decisions about how the home computer is used and where it is placed in the house so it can be supervised. They will have to make decisions in collaboration with the teacher in relation to homework and holidays. Will a holiday be a relaxing break or a learning experience? Will there be access to online learning resources so formal learning can continue at a distance from the classroom?

What are the characteristics of effective learning?

The Hay, McBer Report (2000), *Research into Teacher Effectiveness*, gives a good summary of this.

Characteristics of Effective Learning and Response in Lessons

Pupils:

- sustain concentration
- maintain active involvement (well-motivated, show perseverance, answer questions)
- select and use resources critically
- display a range of learning skills including:
    observing and seeking information
    looking for patterns and deeper understanding
    solving problems

communicating information and ideas in different ways
applying what has been learned in new contexts
evaluating work done
- show capacity for independent work (pose questions, show initiative)
- behave well (dependable, handle materials and equipment carefully)
- collaborate in groups (respect the views of others)
- take responsibility

Characteristics of Effective Learning Displayed in Pupils' Work

Pupils:

- understand what they are doing
- are clear about what needs to be done
- complete the tasks they are set
- respond to the comments of the teacher
- display a range of learning skills including:
    observing and seeking information
    looking for patterns and deeper understanding
    solving problems
    communicating information and ideas in different ways
    applying what has been learned in new contexts
    evaluating work done

How can we make a difference in the classroom today?

- *Change where we sit.* What difference does it make to your feelings towards the children, your influence over them, their feelings about you? Try a different place for a week and reflect on the change.
- *Change where they sit.* It's easy to sort out a seating plan at the beginning of term and leave it there. Consider how you might change seating to accommodate friendship groups, effective team collaboration, individual working. Explain the benefits and be prepared to make changes for different activities. Consider alternating boys and girls.

- *Change the management of the classroom furniture.* Find space for resources and place them centrally, around the edges of the room, or dispersed locally for each table. How does this affect the way the children work?
- *Encourage use of the library/resources centre.* Make it easy for pupils to visit and ensure they have a clear strategy when they arrive.
- *Encourage responsibility with an accepted pattern of permissions without the need to ask you first.* Responsibility, given when it is deserved, leads to trust and to independence.
- *Implement a methodical approach to information literacy and study skills.*
- *Extend your own range of skills* so learning is presented to your pupils in a variety of ways.
- *Encourage everyone to take part.* Offer a range of activities which pupils can choose according to their preferred learning styles. Then push them to extend the range of their styles.
- *Assess pupils according to all their abilities,* not just accepted or traditional skills. Praise them for real achievements across a wide range of attitudes, skills and personality features so they value themselves.

2

FRAMEWORKS FOR INFORMATION LITERACY

Our pupils need to be information literate, lifelong learners to cope with the changes that will take place in their lifetimes.

Samuel Johnson said that:

> Knowledge is of two kinds: we know a subject ourselves, or we know where to find information upon it.
>
> *Boswell (1979)*

While there are these two basic kinds, information now appears in a bewildering range of formats. Electronic files come on many different media (disks, CD ROMs, DVDs), as Web pages, as databases. Information comes via television, film, radio (accessible online too) and we also have the traditional periodicals, leaflets, newspapers and, let's not forget, books.

Where we have traditionally taught reading, use of contents and indexes, perhaps searching and scanning, we now have to consider the skills of accessing the new media. ICT-mediated learning requires ICT skills and advanced search techniques as well as processing the results.

Where we have traditionally taught speaking, listening and letter writing, we now also have to consider how best to use email, threaded discussions, global online collaborations, video conferencing, interactive media, attachments, simultaneous chat and text-to-speech and speech-to-text processing.

What is described as a 'media-rich' environment could equally be described as 'info glut', where huge mounds of data of uncertain provenance are expanding into larger piles of info garbage.

These are new media, new ways of communicating which we have to adapt to and exploit if we are to keep up with the vast outflow of data.

We may, rightly, complain that we are suffering from information overload, but teachers and librarians – preferably working together in schools – are the people who can help the next generation overcome the problem. If not, who else will do it?

> It has been demonstrated that, when teachers and librarians work together, students achieve higher levels of literacy,

reading, learning, problem-solving and information and communication technology skills.

UNESCO/IFLA School Library Manifesto (2000)

We have always required the skills of asking appropriate questions, searching for sources, extracting relevant information and presenting it in the most effective form. Now the Internet has massively expanded the quantity (if not the quality) of information available to us, and computers have provided us with the tools to make some sense of this mountain of electronic data.

The solution is not a self-contained IT lesson, but a much broader approach to using computers as tools and towards information literacy, which integrates with all that we do in schools. These are the skills of today and of tomorrow.

Computers are no longer just in the hands of the privileged or the fortunate, they are necessary tools for everyone. They long ago stopped being academic or technical tools; they are now the gateway to knowledge for all.

The unemployed looking for a job must use a computer and use information strategies to scan, sift, compare and evaluate the information. The small businessman and sole trader must fill in tax returns, maintain databases and a website, then generate invoices – all using a computer.

Every time we use the Internet to browse possible holiday destinations, find a bed and breakfast, use a dating agency, trawl for bargains, do our online shopping, sell superfluous goods, read the news, delete our spam email, buy music or DVD entertainment, we make some use of our information literacy skills.

And if we find ourselves with a thousand holidays but none at the right time, a meeting with a prospective partner who doesn't match our specification, a cheap MP3 player with the wrong socket, a DVD with the right title but the wrong actors or an attachment bearing a killer virus then we wish we had higher level skills.

Learning those skills starts with teaching the teachers and ends with learning to learn.

The rest of this chapter offers frameworks which already exist to try to make sense of the overwhelming number of skills needed to change data into information and make sense of the information glut.

Information literacy

Information Literacy is the ability to locate pertinent information, evaluate its reliability, analyse and synthesise the information to construct personal meaning and apply it to informed decision making.

Berger (1998)

There is a necessary balance between knowledge and knowing how to find out – between having key facts in your head, having the understanding of how to use them, and having the skill to draw on extra resources too.

Information literacy is as important as traditional reading literacy and it incorporates a wide range of skills which are essential in the modern world. Many of the skills already feature in the national curriculum, though because they are not usually brought together, too often there is no coherent approach to how they are learned. They are relevant to every teacher and every pupil; they feature in every one of the National Curriculum subject areas; they are cross-curricular in every sense – yet because they belong to everyone they are owned by no one.

Whether you choose one of the following frameworks or create your own from the best bits of each, I believe these skills must be taught to every child in every school.

The skills words used in the National Curriculum

Ask	Refine search methods	Scanning
Be systematic	Investigate	Summarize
		Record

Collect	Develop	Analyse
Identify relevant sources	Explore	Interpret
Select		
Reorganize	Present	Evaluate
Adapt	Communicate	
Modify	Use graphic techniques	
	Draw conclusions	

The research and study skills strand of the National Literacy Strategy

Pupils should be taught to:

Year 7

1. know how to locate resources for a given task, and find relevant information in them, e.g. skimming, use of index, glossary, key words, hotlinks
2. use appropriate reading strategies to extract particular information, e.g. highlighting, scanning
3. compare and contrast the ways information is presented in different forms, e.g. web pages, diagrams, prose
4. make brief, clearly organized notes of key points for later use
5. appraise the value and relevance of information found and acknowledge sources

Year 8

1. combine information from various sources into one coherent document
2. undertake independent research using a range of reading strategies, applying their knowledge of how texts and ICT databases are organized and acknowledging sources
3. make notes in different ways, choosing a form which suits the purpose, e.g. diagrammatic notes, making notes during a video, abbreviating for speed and ease of retrieval

Year 9
1. review and extend their own strategies for locating, appraising and extracting relevant information
2. synthesize information from a range of sources, shaping material to meet the reader's needs
3. increase the speed and accuracy of note-making skills and use notes for re-presenting information for specific purposes
4. evaluate the relevance, reliability and validity of information available through print, ICT and other media sources

While most of the learning skills of information literacy, study skills and thinking skills are agreed, the language to express them does differ. The list below brings together the terminology and the skills to cover aspects of thinking, studying and learning.

1.	Formulate/Ask questions	Define, specify tasks	Identify appropriate learning strategies
2.	Identify sources	Brainstorm all possibilities	
	Locate/find sources	Collect/gather sources	Retrieve
3.	Interrogate resources: read for meaning, listening skills, visual skills	Use appropriate book techniques: contents, index, glossary, Dewey	Scan/skim, speed reading
	Search, use key words and advanced search techniques	Select, discriminate, reject	Evaluate relevance reliability, appropriateness and authenticity of resources
4.	Interpret and understand	Record, note	Summarize/précis

5.	Use appropriate ICT skills: word-processing, text manipulation, presentation, multimedia, hypertext	Synthesize, combine	Analyse
	Organize, arrange, sort *(mind mapping, tables, hyperlinks graphic organizers such as tables for and against)*	Repurpose/adapt /modify	Avoid plagiarism
	Edit	Write in appropriate styles for a given purpose or audience	Acknowledge sources
	Present, communicate, graphically and linguistically *(oral, written)*		
6.	Conclude	Evaluate outcome	Reflect

These are skills of information literacy. How can we organize them into a coherent framework?

Methodical frameworks

'Finding out' sounds such a simple thing to do – yet it is a complex suite of skills, each of which must be learned before it can be used in combination with the other skills. It is so easy to cut corners and end up with the wrong answer, or follow a promising route but end up with an inappropriate solution.

I believe these are essential life skills. They are already embedded in the National Literacy Strategy and the National Curriculum so they are not additional to our current responsibilities. However they are being lost among so many other learning objectives that I feel they deserve attention.

How can we teach them?

A practical answer is first to devise a methodical and memorable set of stages to guide us through the necessary skills. The lists of skills above, including near synonyms and inter-pretations, may seem overwhelming.

The ideal would be to identify a few stages which are so detailed that they can cope with any information-related task, yet simple enough for everyone to use and short enough to be memorable. They would be written in language which is clear and unambiguous, yet allow for flexibility in how the user carries them out. They would appeal to users irrespective of their preferred learning styles, age and competence, and be so self-evidently useful that they would painlessly unlock the answers to all questions and the solutions to all problems.

Is there such a universal method? It would be hard to find anything in the world to appeal to everyone, but there are several possible candidates for best information literacy method. Look through the methods below and think about which one you would want to use.

Which methodical plan?

Take a look at each in turn, and also consider why it might be useful to develop your own.

The Eisenberg/Berkowitz Big Six model of information problem-solving (Eisenberg/Berkowitz 1990)

1. Task Definition
1.1 Define the task (the information problem)
1.2 Identify information needed in order to complete the task (to solve the information problem)

2. Information Seeking Strategies
2.1 Brainstorm all possible sources
2.2 Select the best sources

---

3. *Location and Access*
3.1 Locate sources
3.2 Find information within the source

4. *Use of Information*
4.1 Engage in the source (read, hear, view, touch)
4.2 Extract relevant information

5. *Synthesis*
5.1 Organize information from multiple sources
5.2 Present the information

6. *Evaluation*
6.1 Judge the process (efficiency)
6.2 Judge the product (effectiveness)

The Nine Question Steps (LISC 1985)

1. What do I need to do?	(formulate and analyse need)
2. Where could I go?	(identify and appraise likely sources)
3. How do I get to the information?	(trace and locate individual resources)
4. Which resources shall I use?	(examine, select, reject individual resources)
5. How shall I use the resources?	(interrogate resources)
6. What should I make a record of?	(record and sort information
7. Have I got the information I need?	(interpret, analyse, synthesize, evaluate)
8. How should I present it?	(present, communicate)
9. What have I achieved?	(evaluate)

Nine Stages

Stage 1:	What does this mean?	(comprehension of the task)
Stage 2:	What must I do to answer this?	(deciding upon an approach)
Stage 3:	What can I use to help me?	(selection of resources)
Stage 4:	Where is the relevant information?	(using the resource, contents, index)
Stage 5:	What does this mean?	(comprehending the information)
Stage 6:	What should I use?	(selection of relevant points)
Stage 7:	How should I organize this for presentation?	(organization of notes)
Stage 8:	Presentation	(design and delivery)
Stage 9:	Have I done it properly?	(evaluation)

The Hinchingbrooke Six-Step Plan (Devised at Hinchingbrooke School, Huntingdon, 1990)

Ask
Find
Choose
Do
Answer
Reflect

Five Steps to Research Success (Adapted from Bloom's Taxonomy by Winebrenner 1992)

Plan   (task, questions, purpose)
Find   (resources)
Work   (with the information)
Present   (the finished product)
Reflect   (how well did I do, what did I learn about both the subject and about researching, what could I do better next time?)

Three Big Steps

Preview
Do
Review

The Three Big Steps is a synthesis of the longer lists, suitable for younger children and for a quick fix.

The PLUS model of information skills (Herring 1999)

Purpose
Identify the purpose of your research. Write it as a question or a clearly expressed task. The task may have several sections to it but describe each one clearly.

Location
Find relevant information sources related to the purpose. Are they correct, up to date, in a useful medium?

Use
Select and reject information and ideas, read for information, make meaningful notes, present your answers appropriately.

Self evaluation
Did you succeed? Did you do as well as you wanted? Did you learn anything? Did you present your answers successfully?

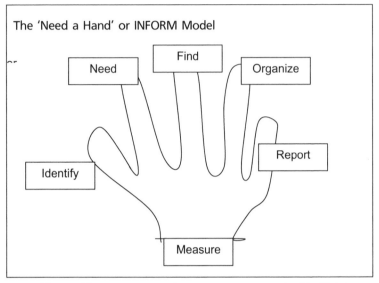

The 'Need a Hand' or INFORM Model

Created by participants at a course by Duncan Grey, organized by Lighthouse Training, London (March 2004).

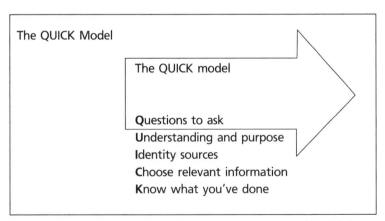

The QUICK Model

The QUICK model

Questions to ask
Understanding and purpose
Identity sources
Choose relevant information
Know what you've done

Created by participants at a course by Duncan Grey, organized by Lighthouse Training, London (June 2005).

The GNVQ method

1. Design an action plan
2. Identify information needs
3. Seek information
4. Select information
5. Synthesize
6. Communicate effectively
7. Evaluate

You may find that elements of each model appeal to you but you can't wholeheartedly adopt any one method. Consider what you like or dislike about each of the above models before reading my comments below.

One brief analysis would be:

Big Six	Six steps would be great but this is 12. However, lots of support at http://www.big6.com/
Nine Question Steps	Excellent stages but too many to remember easily. A good guide to the process but needs simplifying.
Nine Stages	Too many and too many alternatives A good guide to the process but needs simplifying.
Hinchingbrooke	Unclear difference between 'do' and 'answer'.
Five Steps	Misses out the crucial stage of selection and choosing.
Three Big Steps	Beguiling simplicity but not detailed enough for advanced research.

PLUS	Memorable acronym but 'use' is not effectively defined.
Need a Hand/INFORM	Great picture and acronym, but 'need' and 'measure' don't work.
QUICK	Great acronym, though omits 'do' or 'answer'.
The GNVQ method	Uses clear terminology except for the Action Plan which complicates it by referring to another kind of method.

If you like one of the methods above that's great – go and implement it now! But if you don't find one that's perfect, why not cannibalize them and create your own?

Working at Hinchingbrooke School in Huntingdon, I formed a working party with representatives from each subject department. We looked at the models above and then we designed our own. Whether it is better than existing models or not is less important than the fact that we created it for ourselves and we therefore had 'ownership' of it. This is the best model of all.

Before long the Hinchingbrooke Six-Step Plan for information literacy was translated into several languages and being used in the modern foreign languages department, was printed on large coloured sheets and hung on the walls of the resources centre, was stuck on the walls outside the Middle School toilets (everyone will see it as they walk past, sir!) and inserted into every pupil's day book.

In due course the Six-Step Plan was being built into research tasks and projects throughout the curriculum. And it was working not because the steps were the best information handling strategy in the world, but because they had been created by the teachers themselves. Instead of having something imposed upon them they had created something of their own.

3

INTEGRATING
INFORMATION
SKILLS INTO THE
CURRICULUM

Pushing the agenda onwards

Some educational innovations fade away after the initial enthusiasm. The initial energy is lost, the bright young things and high fliers move on and up and leave behind little piles of documents and policies which never quite made it but looked good on their CVs.

I'm determined Information Literacy is not going to go the same way! It is vital that these information skills are securely embedded in the curriculum, that they are visited and revisited by all teachers, all pupils, every year group. These are skills our pupils need for their futures and we need to make sure they have learned how to learn.

So here are some strategies for making sure we embed information literacy in the daily life of your school. At the end of this chapter is a list of Twenty-Five Tips which you could keep with you to check your progress, and a sample information literacy policy for your school.

The spiral curriculum

The information skills curriculum is spiral or recursive. I have represented this with the following picture. The five fingers relate to the Five-Step Plan and the spiral in the palm refers to the spiral curriculum.

For example, in Year 8 pupils will revisit the idea of the accuracy of information and look closer at the evidence of inaccuracy.

In Year 9 they will start looking at the subtler forms of persuasion and prejudice which skew information.

In Year 10 they may create several versions of biased material based on core information and write a commentary on what they have done.

At each turn of the spiral pupils look at information in a more detailed and mature way.

Take every opportunity to create the work around an information skills framework, to inject information skills

activities into existing work and to note where information skills already exists. The information skills learned here will make children's learning more effective.

Advertise the vital steps of information handling throughout the school. Make this especially prominently in the LRC and attach/relate the Plan to a wide range of events, such as:

Planning a holiday
A shopping trip
Repairing a bicycle puncture
Choosing your university/Year 9 options for GCSE
Designing a school website
Redesigning the school

Include the Plan in pupils' day books and inside back covers of curriculum materials, on bookmarks and stickers.

Design the Plan to suit the subject area – translate into modern foreign languages, link graphically to a scientific experiment, geography investigation, etc.

Keep plugging it – by the time some people are tired of it others will have hardly adopted it. Do bring out tea and biscuits, coffee and chocolate, even wine and cheese to bring people together and revive interest! Provide occasional bulletins of recent successes or details of how information skills are important enough to feature in world news (it prevented a plane crash, it traced a terrorist, it revealed my family tree . . .).

Keep checking and monitoring it – make sure the Plan is being carried out. Ask pupils and teachers informally first, and check revised curriculum plans to ensure it doesn't slide off the agenda. Also check that the Plan is understood by new teachers and is being taught at the depth and level you need. After all, cursory teaching at an early stage could affect effectiveness elsewhere in the curriculum.

There are two ways in which we can check that our pupils are learning information skills effectively. First we can give them a brief assessment during activities which we know make use of information skills. I'm thinking of a three-point scale where + means doing well, 0 means coping OK, and x means not doing well. You could assess the individual skills (as described in Chapter 4) in this way to build up a profile of information skills, then set individual activities for particular skills if these need attention. I think this is easier to cope with and more likely to be effective than tests or examinations. The second and surest way to check that using these skills is having an effect is to continue to use them in every area of the school.

Putting it all together

I've identified many features of a successful Information-Centred Curriculum. To sum up, here are nine main features:

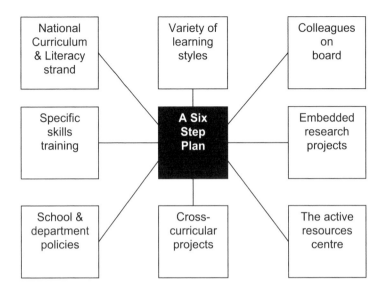

Your school's information skills strategy will incorporate all these features. It will do so by adopting a methodical information skills scheme, probably of six key steps. This will be official school policy, embedded in all departments' teaching schemes of work and taught by relating information skills to the normal subject content. Specific skills will be taught first discretely, then integrated into subject areas in a variety of situations and using a variety of approaches and learning styles.

All teachers will be aware that other teachers are following the same scheme, therefore reinforcing their own work, and will appreciate how this follows the National Curriculum and Literacy Strategies.

Pupils will be explicitly aware of the coherent thread running through their lessons. They will see the Six-Step Plan on classroom walls and in their day books. Some classes will come across information skills in traditional classroom teaching, some in cross-curricular projects, some when they visit the library resources centre for their frequent research activities. Parents will be aware of the strategy and those who are willing may come to a parents' evening and reinforce the Six-Step Plan at home in practical situations. Ofsted will be amazed. The director of studies ecstatic. The head will give you a rise. You will be typically modest about your great achievement.

Twenty-Five tips

1. Collect your own information literacy resources, such as the list of methods above.
2. Define 3 really good reasons why your school should take on this approach.
3. Talk to a sympathetic line manager and gain support.
4. Talk to sympathetic colleagues and gain their support. Convince them that this is a Good Idea.
5. Try out some small-scale projects and lessons where research methods can be taught methodically or where individual information skills can be learned.
6. Introduce your Good Idea to the head and the head of curriculum. Convince them that it should be a whole-school policy.
7. Introduce your Good Idea to the staff at a training day.
8. Have presentations by staff who support you and who have made information skills work in their lessons.
9. Offer a learning skills inventory to all staff followed by a discussion about what is meant by learning styles and how this links to information literacy.
10. Chair a cross-curricular working party to agree on a school information method – a Five- or Six-Step Plan to be used across the whole school.
11. Identify what skills need to be taught, who is going to teach them and when.
12. Emphasize the use of the resources centre as a gateway to learning resources and the ideal place for collaborative, resource-based and computer-mediated learning.
13. Have your working party compile and approve a whole-school information handling policy, to cover the curriculum and the school's administration.
14. Hold assemblies demonstrating how information skills and a variety of learning styles can solve everyday problems.

---

15. Collect examples of best-practice curriculum activities across the curriculum.
16. Advertise the school information method everywhere around the school, with relevant examples of its advantages. Include the school canteen as well as the classrooms and common areas.
17. Explain the method to governors.
18. Advertise the school information method in the parents' bulletin and hold a meeting to explain it and show how it will be useful at home.
19. Add it to all pupils' day books.
20. Review all projects and activities and revise them to include reference to the school information method. Make sure the five-step framework is the backbone of worthwhile curriculum projects which are being taught for their intrinsic merits.
21. Provide training sessions and aim to get every teacher and every department familiar with the overall concept of information literacy and capable of teaching at least some of the information skills which are relevant to their subject area.
22. Have the school adopt an information literacy policy.
23. Work with the curriculum deputy to create a spiral model of the curriculum in which Information skills are taught methodically early then revisited and built upon every subsequent year.
24. Have this approved and agreed by the school and enshrined in their individual and collective policy documents.
25. Don't give up! If it was worth starting, it's worth going on. If some of the early adopters fall by the wayside that will be balanced by the later arrivals on the bandwagon!

A school information skills policy

Recognizes that:

A common methodical approach to information handling is a real benefit for teaching and learning.

That the information skills thread which runs through all subjects in the National Curriculum is a valuable source of guidance and provides a checklist for all subject areas.

That the skills of information handling are best taught within the existing curriculum framework.

That specific skills may best be taught first in certain subject areas before embedding in the whole curriculum.

That all staff have a duty to teach and reinforce information skills in their teaching and that by doing so we help each other and create more effective learning for our pupils.

We agree that:

Each teaching department includes references to use of the learning resources' centre and to teaching information skills in their curriculum.

Copies of these curriculum documents should be available to all teachers and specifically the deputy head of curriculum and the librarian.

A copy of the school Information skills framework should be printed in the school day book for every pupil.

A working party comprising representatives of every subject area be formed with the objectives of:

- – agreeing on a methodical skills framework
- – ensuring that all subject areas are teaching information skills
- – identifying areas where information skills are particularly emphasized
- – spreading good practice of information skills use
- – identifying which departments will teach specific skills and techniques and where these will appear on the curriculum
- – carrying out a regular inventory of information literacy within the curriculum

An appendix to the policy would include:

Five/Six-Step Plan
List of specific information skills
National Curriculum Information Skills Thread document

4

INDIVIDUAL LEARNING SKILLS

> Our sons and daughters will not hew, forge,
> mine, plough or weld. They will serve, design,
> advise, create, compose, analyse, judge and
> write.
>
> *Charles Leadbeater (2003)*

There may be an infinite number of learning skills, many of which will overlap, but here are what I see as the most important learning skills. These skills:

- are an essential part of information literacy
- can be taught discretely
- can be embedded in other learning activities
- are modest yet vital building bricks in the overall information literacy structure

See also the study skills in Chapter 5.

Asking the right questions

How do we know which are the right questions to ask? That in itself is a very fair question ...

One way is to show by example. After all, teachers are always asking questions so surely they will be best at demonstrating successful questioning techniques.

Good and bad questions

'The only stupid question is the one you don't ask'. But there are ways of encouraging questions in the classroom and ways of avoiding awkward answers.

Closed questions

- May elicit recall: e.g. 'What is an escarpment?' 'What is the number of this element in the periodic table?' 'Who was the President in 1945?'

Effective quick-fire questions can increase alertness and test understanding, though they don't actually develop learning in themselves.

- They may also be a bungled attempt to increase teacher–pupil interactivity: 'What do you think he was called?' 'Does anyone have any ideas?'

  These include 'Guess what teacher is thinking' questions and involve pupils hazarding random guesses in the hope of hitting a target which pleases teacher – or not.

Open questions

- Can stimulate discussion and imagination, especially if they are building on shared knowledge and experience.

  Stopping a narrative at a crucial moment and asking 'What happens next?' can cause pupils to combine their knowledge of events and characters so far and imagine possible developments.

- Can stimulate the imagination and could be the basis for a creative project.

  Asking for possible uses for a brick or what use a castaway might make of a ball of string, a plastic carton, a car tyre and a wooden crate (for example).

- Avoid too many broad or vague questions and vary the people you are addressing.

  Does anyone know anything about the Civil War? Balance this with either 'Who can tell me about the causes of the Civil War?' and 'James, tell me what you know about the causes of the Civil War.'

- Try to target pupils with questions they are likely to be able to answer.

  This is differentiation and need not be condescending.

Organizational questions

These should

 - narrow down the number of possible responses
 - be well focused and targeted
 - aim to limit simultaneous calling out
 - be rephrased as instructions rather than questions, where possible

Don't ask 'Does anyone need a ruler?' 'Does everyone understand?'
Do ask 'Who does not have a ruler?' 'Is there anyone who does not understand?'
Don't ask 'Is there anyone away today?'
Do ask 'Put your hand up if you think there is someone from this class not here today.'

Disciplinary questions

Don't ask 'Where do you think you're going?'
Do ask 'Where should you be?'
Don't use sarcasm: 'Do you want to poison us all?' 'How do you expect to write without a pen?' 'Were you brought up in a field?'
Do ask: 'Turn off the gas tap. That's dangerous', 'Bring in a pen for next lesson', 'Please close the door.'

The black attaché case

Another way of looking at it is to use Frank Miceli's classic black attaché case. Pupils are invited to think about questions which they think are worth answering.

The teacher brings in a black bag and tells the pupils they have a special computer capable of answering any question anyone asks. When a wide variety of questions has been listed, the teacher then says that the computer is expensive to operate and

45

that it would be wasteful to use it for answers we already know. The group now looks at the list and eliminates those questions where the answers are easily discovered (how old am I, when is my mum's birthday).

Next the teacher says the computer has difficulty with questions which are worded vaguely or imprecisely (how much information is there in the world, what do we mean by information, how do we count it, when do we start and stop counting? ...).

While Miceli's pupils soon realized the computer was not miraculous, they realized that analysing questions was a worthwhile task – and continued with it, insisting that the case was there every time!

They evolved their own set of questions about questions which helped someone to know:

- what they were talking about
- what sort of information was required
- whether or not a question can be answered
- what we must do to find an answer if there is one.

McKenzie and Bryce Davis (1986) also suggest that pupils identify different kinds of questions. 'They may come up with types such as "Fact Questions" and "Why Questions" and "Imagine Questions." Or they may find other names. It does not really matter, for the important thing is to start them thinking about questions.'

The Holy Grail

Deceptively simple questions feature in *Monty Python and the Holy Grail* (1975). It is worth playing the short scene where Arthur and his Knights try to cross the Bridge of Death.

Who would cross the Bridge of Death must answer me these questions three.

The questions are 'What is your name?', 'What is your quest?' (everyone is asked these) and 'What is your favourite colour?' (this third question always varies).

The first and second questions require absolute answers which the person being questioned already knows. The third however is an opinion and rather more difficult to define. If I say 'blue', I may be correct today but I may have changed my mind tomorrow. And how can the questioner know whether I'm telling the truth or not?

Sir Lancelot answers his questions without difficulty, but an overconfident Sir Robin finds his third question is 'What is the capital of Assyria.' Unable to answer he dies a dreadful death.

The answer to this question is far more complex than it appears. Sir Robin might have replied, 'It depends on your meaning of Assyria', because the geographical location of what we call Assyria changed several times between the second millennium BC and AD 610. At various times its capital was Ashur, Nineveh, Kalakh and Dur Sharrukin. Perhaps Sir Robin should have requested clarification of the question, which would have sent the Guardian to an untimely death.

Sir Galahad, unable to decide *his* favourite colour, meets a similar awful death (moral: be decisive). However King Arthur, faced with the question 'What is the airspeed velocity of an unnamed swallow' confidently throws the question back to the questioner – 'What do you mean, African or European swallow?' Unable to answer the question himself, the Guardian of the Bridge is himself condemned to die.

And the moral of this story is:

- distinguish between fact and opinion
- if you don't know, have strategies ready to enable you to find out
- clarify the question – what does it really mean?

Perhaps the ability to ask the right questions really is the Holy Grail. Perhaps asking the right question actually is a matter of life and death.

Defining the task

Who, what, why, where, when and how are good prompt questions to check whether all avenues have been covered.

- *Who* has asked for this? (who do I ask if I have questions later, who do I give it to); *Who* is going to do it? (all of us, some of, just me, with or without help . . .)
- *What* precisely do I have to do? (what does it involve in terms of time, effort, length, detail . . .)
- *Why* am I doing this? (is it assessed coursework, is it essential to the course or background work, is it voluntary or compulsory, will it lead to other activities . . .)
- *Where* are the materials and resources? Where do I have to deliver the final product?
- *When* must it be done by? (deadlines and what to expect if it isn't completed in time, should I start it straight away or will we do some preparation first . . .)
- *How* should it be done? (formal written essay or multi-media project, are there guidelines on what is advised and recommended for how it is presented . . .)

However, they are not the only question types. Add

- what if . . .
- suppose
- in what ways might . . .
- would you rather . . . or . . .

to broaden the scope for thought and stimulate imagination.

Teachers should check there is no ambiguity in the task description and provide examples where possible. There are pupils who will simply not understand what you tell them, others who will wilfully misunderstand whenever possible, and others who will wriggle out of any hard work unless the instructions are watertight.

The teacher's art here is to allow creative flexibility in the way the task is done (using a variety of media, different learning styles) but to be strict about the quality of the product. It may be necessary to define the number of words written, time spent or pages produced, though it may be possible to encourage a variety of means of reaching the goal.

Making predictions, testing theories, analysing results, problem-solving

These skills relate to the science and mathematics curricula, though they can equally apply to a process in design technology or geography, a 'what if' situation in history and a narrative in English. They work best where pupils are given a problem, think broadly about it first, narrow their options by selecting and discarding, and finally choose a single solution.

Putting this solution into practice, they can then test the effectiveness of it and collate evidence on how effectively they solved the problem. By definition a scientific experiment will involve this skill, but non-scientists can also try:

- Read *Romeo and Juliet* up to the point where Romeo leaves the party and Juliet discovers who he is. What will happen next? Discuss possible actions and endings. Base your discussions on textual evidence from Act I only.
- Design a chair for use by older people attending outdoor events – low enough not to obscure the view for others, comfortable enough for sitting on for a long time, light, small and strong enough to keep in a car boot and carry safely to the event. Try out existing models against this brief. Try to make a better one yourself.
- Draw a road layout for your local area. Add junctions and obstacles and predict how these will alter the flow. Use Technics Lego or suitable software to create the road layout with traffic lights controlling traffic flow. Compare your predictions with the results from the model.

- Describe a battle, significant event or political decision but stop before the consequences become clear. Discuss possible scenarios such as the introduction of more horses/archers/ tanks or changes in terrain or weather. How would this change things? Compare with the actual event.
- Using an infrared keyboard and data projector or a whiteboard, the class can play a quest game such as *Myst* or a simulation game such as *Sim City*. The teacher can facilitate discussion and choice, encouraging the whole class to take part in decision-making.
- Spreadsheets are perfect 'what if' devices. Create a spreadsheet for the costs of food for a party and calculate how much lemonade, how many bags of crisps, etc. will be needed for 15 people. Then change the number of people, the timing of the party, the cost of the items, etc. and discuss what is likely to happen. The spreadsheet will show the consequences.

Genuine problem-solving on school issues is also feasible. How do we stop mobile phones disrupting lessons or being used to bully children? How do we make sure everyone gets their work/ play balance right? How do we keep the school litter-free? Real problems require real problem-solving.

Making decisions

A quick guide to decision-making

We all have to make decisions. Most of our decisions are easily made but a few – a very few – need a strategy. Here are some ideas which might help.

Stand back. Take in the wide picture; brainstorm all possibilities before you zoom in on your preferred option.

If you have to decide whether or not, yes or no, this or that, divide a sheet of paper vertically in half and write FOR on one side and AGAINST on the other. Place arguments under each column. Don't forget that it's not just a matter of number but also the quality or importance of the arguments. This is called 'weighing the arguments' and gives a useful image of how we decide on the balance (or imbalance) of a number of arguments.

When it's possible, take time to decide. You must recognize practical deadlines and be decisive sometimes, but don't let someone force you to make an instant decision for their own convenience. 'I'll get back to you' is a reasonable thing to say.

Sometimes it's more important simply that you do decide something than any particular decision you make. This train or that bus? It may make little difference, but if you don't decide at all you'll be stranded!

Share your thoughts with friends. They like helping and can come up with new views. But beware of forceful persuasion in a direction where you feel uncomfortable.

To thine own self be true
And it shall follow as the night the day
That thou shalt not be false to any man

In other words follow your conscience. If you feel uncomfortable about it, don't do it.

Consider your heart as well as your head. In helping a friend to decide you could say firmly, 'I think you should . . .' then turn away. A minute later, ask your friend how they felt when you said it. If their heart has made its own mind up they'll feel it.

It's usually better to be pro-active and make a decision than to let Fate decide for you. Take responsibility for your own life. If you feel at all strongly about something make the decision yourself. Put yourself in the driving seat.

Relax and stop worrying. You may be building this decision into something bigger than it really is. Eat some comfort food, take a bath, zonk in front of *Friends* and you may see things in perspective. Sleep on it. Things are often clearer in the morning. Cultivate a range of things which relax you. Work through real problems but relax into decisions.

Ask yourself – 'Would you rather . . .' and go through a few options.

Don't think it's just you who can't decide – governments, heroes and parents all have the same problems!

Decision-making is built in to the careers route already. Secondary schools start with a broad curriculum and narrow it. Which subject shall I drop and which shall I follow through is an opportunity for decision-making in Years 9 and 11. The decisions need to be informed by asking questions about the course and pupils' personal strengths and aims. They should not be too swayed by previous experiences with teachers in different circumstances, or by the fact that their friends might choose differently.

Brainstorming

A model of the brainstorming process would include both convergent and divergent thinking. First our thinking opens out to include almost anything, however crazy it may first appear. This is divergent.

In due course it begins to focus on the most profitable areas of interest as practicality and necessity take over from open-ended brainstorming. This refining and filtering stage finds the pearl in the oyster. Too much convergence too early and potentially good ideas are excluded; too much divergence for too long and the best ideas are lost in the flood.

Effective brainstorming requires:

- a facilitator to guide and focus the group and to capture the ideas
- a policy of aiming for quantity in the first stage
- a willingness to work together, share, bounce ideas off each other
- an enthusiasm to be playful with ideas
- an agreement to defer judgement

Brainstorming can be an exciting and stimulating classroom activity, though it's important that the hilarious open-ended first stage is followed by the calmer selection and discarding process.

Brainstorming can be part of a team-building exercise with teams competing against each other. Five or six per team is probably the optimum number.

You can relate brainstorming to relevant problem-solving:

- how can we avoid long queues at lunchtime?
- where should we go for a field trip?
- how can we avoid litter on the school site?
- how can we raise money for a new common room?
- how can we individually reduce pollution?

or irrelevant problem-solving:

- how long would it take to move a mountain and how would you do it?
- how might we avoid being hit by meteorites and comets?
- how would you design a new school and a new curriculum for a new world?

You can use it as a stimulus for creativity – think of as many ways as possible for:

- Romeo and Juliet to avoid dying
- Macbeth to be prevented from abusing power
- uses for a brick, an empty film canister, a plastic lemonade bottle

Identifying likely sources

Books and the Internet often seem the best sources of information, but there are many other sources which should be considered. If you're considering planning a holiday, would you prefer a travel website or an aunt recently returned from your chosen place? Each has its advantage and together they may give the most balanced picture.

The following list of sources and media can be made visible in the Resources Centre and used as a checklist for pupils who run to websites without planning their search strategy.

Reference books	Fiction books
Encyclopedias	Websites
Citizens' Advice Bureaux	Counsellors
Friends	CD-ROMs
DVDs	Videos
Audio recordings	Parents
Librarians	Police
Doctors	Teachers
Posters	Films
Local Record Offices	Museums
Art galleries	Television
Radio	Advertisements
Podcasts	

Which of these sources would be useful for: planning a holiday, explaining your spots, explaining the causes of the Civil War, finding a second-hand trombone?

- Which two resources would you take to a desert island to answer all your questions?
- Which single reference source would be most useful if you were trapped in a bomb shelter during a nuclear war?
- If you were trapped in the local historical records office and unable to escape, how would you make best use of the information in there?
- Which resources would still be useful if your electricity was cut off?

Locating individual sources

(Using search engines, catalogues, Dewey, key words.)

Activities which locate individual resources should start with identifying likely sources as above, using different types of search engines and trying different key words.

Search engines

There are three basic types of search engine.

The indexer

Google is arguably the most popular and probably the most powerful search engine. It sends electronic 'bots' to visit the world's websites, stores and indexes them, but does not evaluate them.

You can search *Google* using key words, and using an Advanced Search you can include and exclude particular words and phrases.

The web directory

Yahoo is a web directory. Editors select the information in these directories and arrange it in a hierarchy, from a general top category, down through detailed sub-categories.

You can search *Yahoo* by using key words or by drilling down through the categories, which become more and more specific.

The subject gateway

These are collections of websites arranged under subject headings. They are often selected by experts and you can check the editors or publishers to see if they are credible sources. As they are often selected by individuals it is important to check that they are up to date too.

Search words

Most search engines will ignore words such as 'on the' and 'of'. If it is important that a phrase is found exactly as written, place it in quotation marks.

To be more precise in a search choose *Google Advanced Search* and select whether your search should include all of the words . . ., with the *exact phrase* . . ., with *at least one* of the words . . . or *without* the words . . . .

Library catalogues

These normally work in a similar way to Internet search engines, if you enter appropriate key words. They may also use Dewey numbers and some show the shelf position of the resource.

Library catalogues usually concentrate on books, but many can also index non-book resources including selected websites. A school librarian can therefore complement the book stock by choosing appropriate additional websites.

Key words

Choosing an appropriate key word is a vital skill if you are to achieve a successful search.

Sometimes we need to know more about a subject before knowing enough to choose the best key word, so several searches at different stages in the process can be helpful. Pupils should consider which words are most important and accurate in describing the topic. They should also try synonyms and both singular and plural varieties of words. For example, the key words mathematics, maths and numeracy will produce different search results. This is a good activity, combining English (choosing appropriate vocabulary), mathematics (compiling charts of success rates for searches using different search terms) and information skills (assessing the success of finding appropriate answers to your questions). The activity could cover several search engines and several other media (CD-ROM, encyclopedia, non-fiction index).

Selecting appropriate resources

(Using criteria to select and reject.)

Pupils often believe that more is better in searches. It isn't. Often less is best. Would you rather have a thousand sites of wildly varying quality or a handful which answer your question appropriately? A thousand empty shells or three pearls?

It is tempting to collect lots of answers because *Google* has the power to give them to us, but we need the strength of mind to select only those which are best suited to our needs. And those sources may include books, tapes, disks and people.

After the activity above in 'Locating individual sources – Key words', which experiments with different search words, it's worth discussing how we decide what is the most appropriate answer. Is it satisfactory to choose something which is only just good enough?

- The first essential is to define the task and create a suitable question.
- The second is to be clear about the criteria which define whether the answer you find is appropriate, good enough or the pearl you were looking for.
- A third essential is to be flexible enough to revisit that question if the answer suggests the need.

It might be that the medium in which the answer is found would dictate whether this source is appropriate or not. A digital photograph might be perfect for a talk or visual presentation, but a written answer may be more suitable for use in an examination essay.

Before pupils run off and grab resources heedlessly, it is useful to ask them:

- resources that would not match my needs would be ...
- I would rather have 'x' than 'y'
- I definitely need something which ...

Finding information within the resource

(Search, index, contents, site map, headings, subheadings.)

The best way to interrogate a resource will vary according to the medium. A non-fiction book will probably have an index and contents and we should urge pupils to use these rather than simply flick through pages randomly. A fiction book will require other strategies. A CD-ROM or DVD will be different again.

It is interesting to look at the strategies of finding the meaning of a word in a digital dictionary, in contrast to a traditional printed dictionary. The digital dictionary, either online or on CD-ROM, is much more flexible, with search boxes for key words, Boolean algebra alternatives (and/or/not) and full-text searching, which can turn a good dictionary into a fair book of quotations. The results of the search can then be rapidly copied and pasted into a file for immediate use (copyright notwithstanding).

Not all websites have site maps but these can help searching and can complement web menus.

The whole idea that a book, disk or website needs a structure can be novel to pupils used to dashing off an unstructured piece of writing. Developing a writing framework, offering prepared writing frames and using word processors in outline view can work to help pupils' own writing. Using the style facility in a word processor can help to show the importance of headings, subheadings and paragraphs to define content.

Reading for meaning, comprehension and understanding

This is very much the territory of the English department, which will already be looking at a variety of texts written in different styles. It is, however, worth pointing out that reading online and from a CD-ROM is a different skill from reading a printed page. The way the light reflects or projects; the resolution of the text on a screen (normally 72 dots per square inch while in a book it may be 1000 dpi); the difference between scrolling and page turning; the temptation to browse rather than read ... all this and much more means that the experience and expectations of reading on a screen will be different from reading a printed book.

The resource centre with a balanced menu of books and computers is the ideal place to offer comparisons.

Skimming and scanning

Skimming and scanning are different from browsing.

- *Skimming* involves looking rapidly over a text for the gist or the essence of it.
- *Scanning* involves looking rapidly for key words, searching for a specific answer.
- *Browsing*, at its worst, can be hopping between pages and sites aimlessly, driven by a lack of concentration.

Skimmers get an overall picture and scanners find things they need more quickly; browsers find all sorts of things but rarely what is relevant. The classic scanning exercise is to use two identical phone books or yellow pages books and have pupils race to be first to find a name. In the process they can learn that there are times when reading every word is a disadvantage, and can learn true alphabetical order (including the Mac problem, explained by my phone book thus: 'Names with a prefix Mc are sorted with those beginning Mac').

Searching for a given word in a page of any text gives the

opportunity for a subject teacher to develop skimming and scanning.

The classic skimming exercise is to read a lengthy text in a given (brief) time, then to write a summary of it without referring to it again. Although the art of précis is no longer taught, our information-rich culture needs the skill more than ever. It is said that Margaret Thatcher, while Prime Minister, insisted that no briefing paper should be more than a single side of A4. For a complex issue, that provides a real challenge to a civil servant. Technical and academic reports frequently use Executive Summaries to point out the main conclusions of a long paper and Microsoft Word does offer an AutoSummarize tool. Suffice to say that summarizing a complex issue and writing to a fixed word limit are skills much prized by academics, journalists and civil servants.

Evaluating material – assessing the strengths and weaknesses of sources and resources

(Bias in resources, identifying prejudice and bias, verifying the information, accuracy of website content, accuracy and reliability, distinguishing between fact and fiction, literal and metaphorical meaning, analysis v comment, primary and secondary sources, comparing tables, charts, text, different media.)

Evaluating material in printed form published by a known publisher is less of a problem than assessing the reliability of web sources. While a publisher has a reputation to maintain, selects writers, edits text and maintains quality standards, a website can be created with a minimum of talent, no qualifications and an interest in self-publicity. While a publisher will normally conform to the laws of the land on copyright and libel, an individual could quite easily avoid this by living anonymously in another country or otherwise hoping to avoid responsibility.

It is worth noting that, while public figures, notably the

Archbishop of Canterbury (June 2005), may criticize the wild irresponsibility of web-based media, and describe it as 'close to ... unpoliced conversation', the web is 'an important step in self-empowerment from control by elites. This is why it is feared in China and by dictators everywhere'. (Stott 2005).

A complex set of skills requiring maturity and sensitivity to language is needed to sense subtle emphasis of tone. However, this can also be a detective game for younger pupils, checking on features which reveal whether a source is reliable or not.

In the classroom it can be played out as a courtroom with prosecuting and defence barristers presenting a case which is decided by a judge and jury. 'I put it to you that this resource is prejudiced against meat eaters and the evidence is that ...'

The check list includes:

1. *Authorship* – is the author reliable and knowledgeable? Is there a genuine contact address?
   Language errors may be a sign of a poorly educated author.
   Offensive or exaggerated language may be a giveaway.
2. *Publisher* – is this a recognized body or organization with a reputation and expertise?
   Has the work been published with their approval?
   Is the organization selling or pushing a product, point of view, or is it known to be neutral?
   Check the web address (URL) to see if the work is published personally or on the organization's official web space.
3. *Point of view or bias* – is the author clearly pushing a single point of view or trying to offer a balanced view?
   Is the page supported by a commercial organization with its own point of view?
   Do they recognize that their subject is controversial?
4. *Referral to other sources* – does the author have a biography, bibliography, make reference to other work on the topic.
   Check links and see if they give one point of view or both side of the argument.
5. *Verifiability* – can the information be verified for accuracy? Is there another source to confirm the views of this author?
   Are there criticisms or studies which put across another

point of view? Don't trust the links from the website, do look up other points of view and cross check.

6. *Currency* – when was the work published and when was it last updated? Is the data still relevant?

7. *Design* – the design of a website can give some hints about its origins. Garish colours and outsize typeface may suggest an amateur web designer. However, design is not a reliable guide to content. It could be that an interested and knowledgeable writer has published a very basic website with crude tools. On the other hand a professional company can spend a great deal of money on persuading the reader of an unworthy cause. Compare 'My personal favourite walks' to 'How our tobacco company is helping young people.'

English and history departments will be covering some of this area already so this is a fertile area for anyone looking for inter-departmental cooperation and demonstrating that some information skills are already being taught.

Note-making, précis and summary

(Abbreviating, recording, sifting and sorting, highlighting, avoiding plagiarism.)

The *Trash-N-Treasure* method of teaching note-taking described by Barbara A. Jansen (1996) suggests that pupils should learn to take notes by omitting all words or phrases not essential to the meaning.

This technique could involve highlighting the important bits or scrubbing out the unimportant bits, but either way it requires pupils to read a text and distinguish between useless (trash) and useful (treasure). Discriminating between the two types is of course the greatest skill of all and involves a combination of reading for meaning and having a clear idea of the original question.

Pupils must:

- be accurate and honest
- not distort the author's words
- acknowledge the source of anything they copy

Pupils should ask themselves:

- Does this sentence answer the question that was asked? If yes, it's treasure; if not, it's trash.
- Can I simplify or reduce the length of this sentence without significantly changing its meaning? If yes, cut out the trash and keep the treasure.

Other note-taking strategies

To be used individually or together

1. Underline, highlight or box the most relevant and important words, phrases and sentences.
2. Use these words, phrases and sentences to write succinct sentences which answer the question.
3. Use key words and columns to arrange the information under different headings. For example, for a text about animals choose headings for the animal's qualities – What does it look like? What does it eat? Where does it live? Keep the information brief. Use the information to write a report.
4. Write the topic clearly at the top of the page. Refer back to it often to remind yourself of what you are making notes on.
5. Draw boxes for the six question words: who, what, why, where, when and how. When reading or listening to the text, fill in the boxes with brief relevant information. Use this information to write a report.
6. Demonstrate common abbreviations and symbols. Help pupils to create their own. Abbreviations and symbols save space and make note-making faster and more efficient.

For example	eg
Means	=
More	+
More than	>
Less than	<
Important	*
And	&

Omitting some letters can still leave a word readable:

Station	stn
Road	rd
Television	tv

- There is no need to write in complete sentences
- Use bulleted lists
- Use text-messaging language
- Omit smaller details
- Make a numbered list of the main points
- Use diagrams, graphs or pictures, as well as, and instead of, words
- Copy charts and diagrams accurately where they are given
- Leave spaces between each note
- Write names once, then use initials
- Use green pens when writing, to distinguish between the copied words and your own words

Graphic organizers

(Spidergrams, icons and graphics, coloured highlights, charts and tables, mind maps for brainstorming.)

These are ways of recording and arranging information. Charts and tables are generally in vertical and horizontal grids while spidergrams and mind maps are more flexible, showing connections between ideas.

Both types of graphic organizer are amenable to hand drawing and to computer programs.

Sorting and arranging the data

Contents lists and website menus arrange topics in a logical way and impose order on an intractable mass of information. A table or grid does the same but creates even more regularity, like arranging jelly in a box.

We can use graphical methods to link and arrange facts, ideas and resources in a meaningful way. Making connections between data which were previously separate is a key factor in inventing creating and imagining.

- One popular exercise in creativity is to compose an imaginative story from a short list of unrelated items. You can do this with words on a board or items from a box:
  1. Tell a story which involves the following items: a table, an elephant, a paperclip and a mirror, or
  2. Ask pupils to write down four items, each on a separate piece of paper. Put all the slips in a box, then ask pupils to pull out four items randomly for their story.
- Lists, tables and grids are the simplest graphic organizers. Making notes on an argument is simplified by using this table:

Introduction	
For	Against
Other points	
Summary/Conclusion	

... which then becomes the basis for a report or analysis of the argument.

- Collecting words from a descriptive piece related to the five senses would use five boxes:

Sight	
Sound	
Smell	
Touch	
Taste	

Empty boxes invite pupils to fill them in. An empty box is an effective quick check for teachers that a task has been completed – or not.

- Writing an essay which requires each point to be supported by an explanation and a quotation is best planned by using three columns:

Identify	*Exemplify*	*Qualify*
Birling and the Inspector hold very different views	B: 'We were having a nice little family celebration tonight. And a nasty mess you've made of it now, haven't you?' I: '... a nice little promising life there, I thought, and a nasty mess somebody's made of it.'	The ironic repetition of 'nasty mess' highlights their opposing views – Birling selfishly concerned with his dinner, the Inspector concerned for the loss of life.
Sheila is prepared to admit her mistakes	'It was my own fault' p. 23 'If I could help her now, I would ...' p. 24	We are shown that the younger generation is more likely to admit its errors and more likely to change its ways ...

An alternative stage is to provide pupils with the three-column grid with two of the three columns per row filled in. This provides guidance, while they must work to fill the gaps. Ultimately the grid creates the framework of the essay, with headings and main points becoming paragraphs and subheadings.

Synthesis of data from multiple sources is a key task in processing information. This can be modelled in the classroom in a variety of ways:

- Find half a dozen related facts about a topic. Print these key facts, embedded in paragraphs of text, on several different pieces of paper and give these to small groups of pupils. Also include three or four unrelated paragraphs as red herrings. How long does it take for the group to join up the key pieces of information? Can they answer the key questions – who, what, why, where, when and how?

- Hold a courtroom drama in which one small group questions half a dozen witnesses to find the answers to their key questions. A road traffic accident could have been witnessed by several people who may have interpreted what they saw or partially saw in different ways. Can you piece together the truth of the incident?

- Provide half a dozen contradictory descriptions or reports on a single topic. These could be examples of journalism from two different newspapers, propaganda from different sides in an argument or simply misinformed observations. History classes could find this material easily in different views of the First World War or in the argument over who ordered the Charge of the Light Brigade.

  How can we bring together contradictory views to make an unbiased report?

- A further level of difficulty is achieved if the information you provide lacks a single key fact. In real life the ability to identify what further information is required is most important.

On this last point, being aware that there are things you don't know is an underrated thing. This was expressed by Donald Rumsfeld in an unjustifiably much-mocked speech:

... there are known knowns: there are things we know that we know. There are known unknowns; that is to say there are things that we now know we don't know. But there are also unknown unknowns – there are things we do not know we don't know.

Donald Rumsfeld (2002)

Presenting the data in a structured framework

The tables and grids of information described above act as a framework for a report, essay or presentation.

By organizing it logically and coherently we can make logical connections and link associated ideas so a flow of information is created.

If the end result is to be printed or projected it may gain from being attractive, understandable, and having an appropriate layout and illustrations. A paragraph of comment might be complemented or even replaced by an illustrative chart or diagram, if the message is best explained visually. A complex chart might gain from selective comments and observations. Bullet points might bring out key points and reduce unnecessary descriptive text.

These are design skills as well as language and organizational skills, and need to be taught. They appear in more than one National Curriculum subject.

While there is not the space to deal with it in detail here, examples include:

PowerPoint and other presentation software	A consistent design from slide to slide
	A logical flow from slide to slide
	Selective use of colour to emphasize key points
	Use of no more than 2 fonts and without the combining of italic, bold and capitals
	Use of graphics to convey ideas
	A link to a sound, movie or text file should show the file type

	Fade out old text, highlight new Use animated and flashing effects very sparingly
Web pages	Consistent results from repeated actions: if you click on a right-facing arrow you should progress, click on a house icon you go 'home'. Consistent navigation and clear signposts so you can find your way from one part of the site to another and always easily find your way home.
Charts and diagrams	Tend to start from top left and go to bottom right. If impossible, use arrows and numbers to guide the reader through the process.
Use grids	Professional designers of books, newspapers and web pages use invisible grids to align graphical elements. The grids should help rather than hinder. They give a page shape, stability and consistency.
Use graphics	A picture can be worth a thousand words – but only if it's chosen to illustrate and explain, not if it's to decorate or confuse. Clip art collections can be useful if they have a coherent style, but often your choice of a unique image will be more effective. Remember, most of your audience will have the same clip art collection as you.

Written in clear and accurate language

Using appropriate language – which may be succinct and pithy, or narrative and descriptive – is essential. If the language is spoken we may need to decide on appropriateness of:

- Volume
- Pronunciation
- Speed
- Intonation
- Pitch
- Pauses
- Formality
- Grammar
- Vocabulary

Non-fluency features such as repeated ums and ers or fillers such as 'you know' and 'like' can distract an audience away from otherwise worthy content. Inappropriate grammar can do the same in the spoken or the written form, as can spelling errors. Unfortunately, certain accents generate irritation in some audiences too.

All our research, verification and synthesis of key facts can be worthless if our audience is cringing at infelicities. See presentations using rhetoric, below, for more detail.

Presentations using rhetoric

Rhetoric has had a bad press since it was seen as pompous, insidiously persuasive and insincere. However, the rules of classical rhetoric are immensely useful today in courtrooms, advertising and any presentation or public speech. It is a skill which uses language effectively and can be either sincere or bombastic.

Rhetoric may be used to present a case in the most effective way, showing verbal dexterity. The danger of rhetoric, with its intention to persuade, is that the speaker may 'stretch' the truth and effectively present a worthless or immoral cause.

Rhetoric is: 'That form of speaking which has the intention of making an impact upon, persuading, or influencing a public audience.'

Examples of rhetorical devices

- *Onomatopoeia* (sounds suggest meaning)
- *Metaphor* (a thing is spoken of as being that which it only resembles)
- *Syllogism* (a logical argument in three parts – two premises and a conclusion which follows necessarily from them)
- *Irony* (deliberate use of words to mean the opposite of their literal meaning)
- *Allegory* (a symbolic narrative)
- *Isocolon* (the use of clauses or phrases of equal length)
- *Antithesis* (words balanced in contrast)
- *Anaphora* (repetition of a word at the beginning of consecutive sentences)
- *Hyperbole* (exaggeration)
- *Litotes* (deliberate understatement, especially as a means of expressing modesty in order to gain the audience's favour)

Two basic principles of Socrates

1. The orator should offer a preliminary definition of the nature of his topic.
2. He should divide his subject into its component parts.

The principles of Cicero

The orator:

- must first hit upon what to say
- then manage and marshal his discoveries, not merely in an orderly fashion but with a discriminating eye for the exact weight of each argument
- next go on to array them in the adornments of style
- after that guard them in his memory
- and in the end deliver them with effect and charm.

The formal skills of rhetoric

Invention

1. *Ethos* or proof deriving from the character of the speaker himself. The tone of the speech should establish the speaker's virtue and moral worth.
2. *Pathos* – The emotions induced in the audience. The audience begins to feel that the speaker must be right and is won over to his side.
3. *Logical proof* – Demonstration of the case by means of argument such as syllogisms, examples and maxims.

Arrangement

1. *Introduction* to put the audience in the right frame of mind, e.g. 'Friends, Romans and countrymen ...'
2. *Narration* – a short statement of the facts of the case.
3. *Proposition* – the narrator states succinctly the facts of the case.
4. *Division* – the main headings under which the subject will be treated.
5. *Proof* – the orator marshals all the arguments on his side of the case, giving points in ascending order of importance leading to a climax. This is the core of the argument.
6. *Refutation* – the orator attempts to answer or discredit the arguments advanced against him.
7. *Conclusion*
   a. summing up
   b. amplification – an emphatic statement of the speaker's position, often invoking 'commonplaces' to move the audience to indignation or enthusiasm
   c. an appeal to the audience's tender feelings

Memory

The speech should appear unpremeditated and should, whenever possible, be delivered from memory. Some politicians use translucent electronic screens on which their speech is projected to make it appear as if they are speaking from memory, while in fact they are reading.

Delivery

Use appropriate gestures and facial expressions – the wagging finger of exhortation, the arms and hands spread wide in appeal . . .

The tone of voice may be conversational, intimate or energetic according to subject matter, and given with varied amplification.

Style

1. *Purity* and correctness of language
2. *Clarity* and intelligibility
3. *Decorum* and appropriateness
4. *Ornament*, figures of speech, metaphors, prose rhythm
5. *Questions*
   Interrogatio – a question which requires no answer because it expresses a truth which cannot be denied. This is what is usually referred to as the 'rhetorical question'.
   Rogatio – a question to which we immediately supply our own answer.
   Quaesitio – a string of questions uttered in rapid succession for the sake of emotional emphasis.
   Percontatio – an enquiry in a tone of bewilderment or amazement and allowing no satisfactory or easy reply.

Evaluation and review

Any significant task deserves an evaluation:

- Have I completed the task?
- Have I answered the question?
- Have I done the best I can?
- Have I learned how to do it better next time?

The process of methodical information skills will start with asking the question and defining the task, and must end with evaluation and review of some sort. The process is circular in that we need to check back to the task (hence writing it clearly and boldly in the first place) if we are to check that we have completed it. If we've been diverted and have answered another question, however successfully, we have failed in our mission.

Citing sources (Harvard notation)

The common Harvard standard is as follows:

Author's/Editor's Surname, Initials (Year) *Title* [online] (edition). Place of publication, Publisher (if ascertainable). Available from: URL [Accessed Date]

For example:
Grey, D. S. (2005) Getting the Buggers to Learn (1st edn). London: Continuum.

Quoting websites follows a slightly different pattern:

Grey, Duncan (2004). Plan a Holiday – and follow the six-step plan. Retrieved on 7 August 2005 from the World Wide Web: http://www.putlearningfirst.com/holiday/index.html

One of the reasons for citing sources is to show that pupils recognize they didn't write this piece themselves and they'd like to acknowledge someone else's hard work or good ideas.

Another reason is so that you as teacher can go back to the original to check details.

Plagiarism can be described as 'passing off someone else's work as your own' or as a kind of theft. It's important that pupils understand that apparently free information on the Internet actually belongs to someone. Even if they don't charge you for it, it still doesn't belong to us so we mustn't claim it as our own.

We can avoid plagiarism by:

- setting tasks which require information to be searched for in a variety of sources and media, then assembled into a specified format, e.g.:
  Not 'Find out everything you can about Victorian Times',
  but 'Write a day's entry in the diary of a Victorian child. Describe what you see and do as you go about your day, at home, in the streets and at school.'
- setting original tasks which avoid thoughtless copying or printing
- setting meaningful and thought-provoking tasks
- as part of the task include requirements, such as providing a bibliography that shows you've used at least four different sources and acknowledging those sources.

5

STUDY AND
REVISION SKILLS

Study skills are a kind of information handling skills but they are particularly associated with more formal academic work and examinations. Generally thought of as most suitable for older pupils because they are exam-orientated, it's never too early to start and 'study skills can be fun'!

This chapter has not only advice for teachers but also bullet-point lists of advice for pupils. One of the things that helps pupils in their studying is a list of tips and targets which they can revisit and tick to show they've 'done' something. These lists could be produced for pupils who need reassurance when they're working alone at their revision, or as an aid when helping pupils to prepare for examinations.

Absence and attendance

This may be the most obvious aspect of study, but it's the most important. To learn anything from lessons it's essential to turn up. Whether absence correlates to illness, personal problems, lack of motivation or even alternative worthy activities, pupils who miss lessons do less well in examinations. It is really important that parents and pupils understand this from the beginning.

In addition to collating GCSE and SATS results it is worthwhile showing marks in relation to lesson attendance.

If, despite their best intentions, absence is inevitable, homework should be made available. A stock of 'standing homework' activities relevant to a variety of situations and abilities could be provided by each class teacher or subject department. Made available on the school website, these are ideal activities for non-attenders – even if they are more effective for placating parents than providing for pupils.

Getting the most out of lessons

Suggestions for pupils

Preparation
- Find out what topic or activity you are likely to be covering in the next lesson. Do some reading around the topic beforehand.
- Note down any terms, names or dates which are new to you.
- Note down anything you don't understand.
- Keep your notes up to date.

During the lesson
- Pay attention and concentrate – watch and listen.
- Take part in the lesson (where appropriate).
- Make notes on the main points using headings to identify topics.
- Ask about anything you don't understand.

After the lesson
- Revise your notes after a lesson to make sure there is nothing missing and that you can understand what you have written. This will help you to understand the topic and start your process of planned revision.
- Add any relevant handouts and keep them organized with headings and dates in a folder with dividers.
- Use underlining and highlighter pens to emphasize important features.
- Check quotations and references for accuracy.
- Re-read your notes after a few weeks and make this part of a revision timetable.

Suggestions for teachers

For older pupils prepare a course introductory booklet and discuss it at the first lesson of a new course or module.

This might include:

- Overview of course content by topic
- Assessment objectives
- Advice and warnings
- Key skills required and what skills the course will develop
- Deadlines
- Definitions
- Simple glossary
- Extracts from the formal syllabus
- Examination details
- Recommended reading
- Further sources of information
- Who will teach you and how to contact them

Younger pupils may be told the topic in advance and set simple research tasks to prepare them.

Younger secondary pupils should be advised whether (and how!) they need to take notes, encouraged to do some background reading and research, told if they are to be assessed and how.

Aim to answer the pupil's question 'How can I be more successful in this subject' and offer achievable targets to achieve this.

Interest and Motivation

Pupils

- It's easier to be motivated by a subject that you know will be useful to you and will help you, so think about where you want to go and what you want to do in the future. Get careers advice and find out what's needed, but don't ignore a subject because it doesn't seem to be relevant – you'll limit your options.
- Ask yourself why you find this subject interesting and another not so interesting. Why is your attitude different? Don't blame the teacher or the subject; think about what you can do to make it more interesting to you. If you get a choice of essay titles, topics or course modules, actively choose one that

interests you. A statistics project may be more interesting if you look at football scores; you may be more enthusiastic about making a presentation if it's on a subject you're keen on, so see if it can be done.

- In the end, recognize that some things just have to be worked through and success is getting to the other end.
- Promise yourself a reward if you achieve certain marks or complete certain tasks on time. Some people thrive on incentives and these can be praise from someone you respect, a personal sense of achievement, money or food.
- Guilt and fear of failure are negative motivations, yet can be strong. Ask yourself how your parents, teachers and friends will feel if you fail because you didn't work hard enough. Is that a powerful force in encouraging you to work harder?

Teacher

- Boosting a pupil's self-esteem can make a pupil more confident and capable, and can give them a sense of purpose. It has been said that positive self-esteem is an essential for a fulfilling life.
- Praise given for something done well is healthy and encouraging, but indiscriminate praise devalues and may be worthless ('You're just saying that . . .').
- Aim to praise twice as much as you criticize. Look for positive achievements by pupils everywhere, both in and out of the classroom. However, remember that in an environment where no one fails there may be no motivation to truly succeed.
- Encourage pupils to praise each other and provide opportunities for them to do so.
- It is worth recognizing that guilt and fear of failure can be strong negative motivations. However unfashionable it may be to say so, the desire to avoid disapproval (from peers, teachers and parents) or punishment (extra work, detentions) can be part of a teacher's armoury, used professionally and selectively. Pressure to finish on time and at a high standard can be encouraged by the knowledge that failure will bring criticism or even punishment. And there is no stronger motivation than self-criticism.

- Try peer marking but make sure pupils know this beforehand and show how they can write helpful comments in a positive way. Then reflect on how often you do this yourself in your marking.
- Evaluate projects and extended activities to include 'What have I learned', 'What have I achieved'.
- Cheesy motivational phrases may not be clichés to our pupils as they are to us, so encourage stickers and posters saying 'Foundations Support Learning', 'If a wall is too high, work your way around it', 'Aim high, That's what stars are for'.

Relaxation versus alertness

The balance between relaxation and alertness will be different for every learner, but that's not to say we can ignore it. Too relaxed and we don't give our best, don't have drive or the energy to achieve; too keyed up and stressed and we become too tense or nervous to give of our best.

One simple solution is practice and rehearsal.

Examination practice helps pupils work within structured limits:

- enables the teacher to see how well a candidate can do judged by strict criteria
- provides a great opportunity to identify and feed back strengths and weaknesses
- accustoms the pupil to the unfamiliar sense of isolation and silence of examination conditions
- develops the need to concentrate
- develops examination techniques of writing to a word or time limit, selecting preferences from a range of optional questions, expressing oneself succinctly and accurately, demonstrating one's understanding in response to searching questions.

Used in tandem with coursework, examinations test abilities. We may not enjoy them but they do test us and coping with testing circumstances is a life skill.

Fears and worries

These are inevitable in the face of testing. Physically, our pulse is raised, and we may sweat and display nerves in a variety of ways. Some of this is a result of adrenalin raising our alertness, which helps us cope with stressful events. Panic, displayed by uncontrolled movements, running away or being physically sick for example, is an excessive reaction in the face of examinations. In some cases this can be resolved by medication under supervision, though gradually facing the stress in practice examinations over a period of time is usually a better solution.

Effective study and revision should help alleviate stress, though some of the pupils who react most strongly against stress do so because they are the most conscientious. Positive parental support to help accommodate study revision will help – though parents who say 'it doesn't matter, I was no good at school myself ...' do not help anyone.

Environment and study space

Pupil

- Learning can take place most effectively in conditions where there are no distractions and where there is reasonable comfort.
- Light – use a good even light plus a reading light like an Anglepoise. Light from a window can help, though a view can distract.
- Heat – should be warm enough but not so warm that it becomes soporific.
- Exercise – should be taken regularly. It wakens the brain and warms the body. Ration the breaks and make them a reward for successful working.
- Desk – a desk specially for study is important. Associate the desk with study. Have a small container for pens and pencils.
- Chair – straight-backed and firm, not soft or relaxing.
- Shelves and storage – make all resources such as books and

notes in folders easy to find and close to the desk. Put other things out of view as they will encourage the mind to wander.

Teacher

- Encourage a practical approach to the study environment by having pupils draw their bedroom and design an ideal practical working space.
- Discuss whether music helps study or is distracting.

Revising

Pupil

- Most background reading should already have been done by the time you start revising. Remember re-vising means looking at your work again, not for the first time.
- Use your notes. Make sure they are organized into the different sections covered by the examinations.
- Use previous papers to familiarize yourself with the layout, style and type of questions likely to appear.
- Practise answers to previous questions. Do this in different conditions at different times – 20 minutes just writing notes; slightly less than the full time allocation writing in full; a full day of research and note making followed by 30 minutes of furious writing without notes . . .
- Write a topic heading on a piece of paper and for 20 minutes write everything you know about this topic. Ask yourself 'What have I missed out?' 'What more do I need to know?'
- Write a topic heading and note the top ten points which you have to make about this topic.
- Work alone, in pairs or in small groups. Brainstorm topics and make notes on the ideas other people have, the points they would make in the examination (though check them against research too).
- Active revision is far more effective than passive revision.

Active	Passive
- rearrange notes by topic headings	- reading straight through existing notes
- highlight areas of notes which apply to given topic headings	- copying out existing notes
- choose most important points to use in an essay question	- watching a television programme about the topic
- reorganize notes in priority order	- leafing through notes
- re-enact some of the experiments (safely!)	- trying to recall past experiments
- make a presentation to fellow pupils	- convincing yourself you know the topic
- explain a topic to someone else and answer their questions	- talking to yourself
- practise timed essays	- writing a few lines from time to time

Planning

Pupil

- Planning is mainly about time management. However, it also involves having everything in the right place at the right time without distractions. It's about organization. Just as you need to start off a new course with a new folder and dividers, make sure you have the right equipment for the right occasion.
- Start planning by producing your own kit list. Your personal kit list will be different from the next person's but here's a start:

Bag with pockets and sections	Timetable
Pencil case	Day book/diary
Coloured pens	Library card
Coloured pencils	School IT network password
Pencils (propelling with rubber	Ruler
end is best)	Maths geometry kit
Eraser	Flash memory stick (if permitted)
Black or blue writing pens	Calculator
Notebook	Sharpener
Folder with dividers	
Textbooks, exercise books, PE	
kit, etc. for the day	

Gizmos such as PDAs, palmtops and laptops may be too valuable to risk at school – this will depend on your circumstances.

- Planning might also include an idea of why you're doing this course and what you hope to achieve as a result. At some time you will probably wish you were anywhere except at your desk trying to revise, so keep in mind what you want to do with all this learning.
- Planning may even mean advance planning for a holiday to celebrate your success – something to look forward to.

Teacher

Arrange an exercise where pupils can create (draw or list) their own checklist for exams.

Time management

Pupil

- Plan a calendar of events and key moments well in advance of the examinations. Study the course materials, noting dates of tests and exams, essay delivery dates, etc. Check these don't clash with other important events such as family holidays, celebrations, etc.

- Plan regular low-key revision throughout the course. This makes final revision much less stressful and more effective.
- Plan a balanced routine in the weeks leading up to the exams in which you take account of lessons including 'surgeries' and revision lessons and which provide regular revision time interspersed with leisure and physical activities.
- For course work, aim to have the drafts done well in advance to allow time for amendments.
- Use a computer to produce written course work and start collecting raw material such as articles by others and notes by you. Save these and back them up.
- Always back up important work, preferably on a separate drive or a different medium so you have another copy if the original is destroyed. Uploading files to web space or sending a copy to a parent or friend means you have something to revert to if the worst happens (and it will).
- Allow time for printing out, for mechanical and electronic breakdown. Don't imagine you can use this as an excuse for late delivery, even if it is true!

Teacher

- Provide essential assessment dates at the beginning of courses.
- Remind pupils about the need for regular revision.
- Encourage regular revision by holding regular tests on specific areas of the course.
- Be firm about deadlines and alert parents and tutors if they are not met.

Memorizing and recall techniques

While learning by understanding is more effective and lasting than rote memorizing, there are some things that deserve to be memorized by heart. Simple repetition can help – reading aloud uses the ears to help the memory, and repeated writing or copying can help – but there are other well-established techniques too. A good memory is an advantage in social terms too. Remembering someone's name and perhaps a few key things about them, makes a conversation more personal. The doctor who cannot recall a patient's name or the teacher who can't name a child has lost a vital element of personal relationship.

Memorizing is improved by creating a meaningful relationship between the items being remembered, by understanding what is being remembered, by fitting the new items into previously accumulated knowledge and by organizing the items logically.

We can show this by trying to remember a list of items. Try learning each of these lists in turn. Time yourself as to how long it takes to remember each list effectively.

1. The first set is of nonsense words: WEH, GJA, GYT, YKU, MAK, TOK, FRA, ZAQ, JYT, LPO, KLI, RTG
2. The second set is of standard English words which are unconnected items: daisy, table, beer, rabbit, chair, hamster, rose, wine, dandelion, desk, lemonade, cat
3. The third set is the same as the second but grouped logically:

Flowers	Drinks	Furniture	Animals
daisy	beer	table	rabbit
dandelion	wine	chair	hamster
rose	lemonade	desk	cat

You'll probably find that the third set is easiest to remember because this set has a logical grouping with a meaningful relationship within each column (unlike set 2) and has meaning (unlike set 1).

The lesson for us as teachers is that giving pupils coherent and meaningful information will lead to more effective learning. So a list of 12 random French words will be more difficult to make sense of than 12 words describing a kitchen.

Using the other fact that active learning is always more successful than passive, encouraging pupils to find their own meaning and their own relationships between items could be even more successful.

One useful structure for pupils creating their own meaning is the verbal mnemonic:

One is a bun, 2 is a shoe, 3 is a tree, 4 is a door, 5 is a hive, 6 is sticks, 7 is heaven, 8 is a gate, 9 is a mine, 10 is a hen.

This is itself easily learned because it is a logical progression, has an embedded rhyme and describes easily visualized objects.

Having learned this list it's very easy to associate a list of objects with it, so we might have a bunch of daisies bursting from a bun, a glass of beer nestling in a shoe, a table hanging from a tree, a rabbit-shaped door, etc. The more incongruous the better because new and unusual items have more impact on the memory than mundane things.

- *Mnemonics* – rhyme, rhythm

  Thirty days hath September
  April, June and November
  All the rest have 31 ...

  I before e
  except after c
  when the sound is ee

- *Acronyms* – ROYGBIV for the colours of the rainbow (red, orange, yellow, green, blue, indigo, violet). Let pupils create class acronyms for processes and lists of items. Hang them up in the classroom and refer to them during lessons.
- *Visualization* – play Kim's Game to develop a 'photographic' or visual memory. Take a number of objects, leave them in view while pupils try to remember them, then cover them and see what they can remember. Play this individually or in groups, with varying numbers of objects and a varying amount of viewing time. Repeat Kim's Game but take away a single object and see if the pupil can spot the missing item.
- *Chaining* – this is a form of visualizing which makes it easier to remember several items in order. Link the items together by thinking of images that connect them. So the words shoe,

battery, flower and book might be connected visually in your mind by imagining a shoe using a battery to light its way, the battery illuminating a flower in the dark and the flower as a bookmark for a storybook.

- *Repetition* – one way to turn short-term memory into a long-term memory is by revisiting and repeating. Simple repetition of a list can be useful but using several senses can be more effective. Repetition aloud not only rehearses a string of items but hearing the list spoken is a further reinforcement. Similarly, drawing the items uses the powers of sight. Playing 'I went on my holidays and I took with me ...' is an effective repetition game as each person repeats the list then adds a new item. Meanwhile the whole group hears the list repeated time after time, each time an item longer.

Incidentally, recalling a series of items in reverse can also help memorization. Remembering a lengthy sentence in a foreign language, first say the last word or phrase, then add the previous word or phrase to precede it, etc., gradually building up the sentence from the end until you reach the beginning.

- *Repurposing, recreating and giving context* – beyond repetition, creating a song or a rhyme involves making personal meaning from a list of otherwise characterless items as well as reinforcing the memory by repetition. By drawing the items and creating a personal picture, fitting the items into a song, story or short performance, the items are brought to life and have a more meaningful context.

- *Patterns* – organizing and arranging. One traditional memory trick, called the method of loci, is to associate new items with a previously learned route or place. Provide the opportunity for pupils to memorize either their route to school or a number of objects in their favourite room. Then give them a list of items which they can associate with the places on the route or the objects in the room. Have them place them together in their mind so they can recall them easily. Let them test each other and repeat to improve their ability to recall more and more items for a longer period of time.

- *Chunking* – just as a large meal or a lengthy book is broken down into smaller pieces to make it more digestible, so a series of numbers, for example, is easier to recall in chunks of 3 or 4 rather than as 7 or 8.

- *Physical memory* – whether you read out a list of words and pupils have to run to fetch key items, or if they have to physically sort objects by moving them around, there will be a physical memory attached to the word and this is more powerful than simply hearing or reading it. I hear and I forget, I see and I remember, I do and I understand. Doing could be running after something, moving it or drawing it – activity stimulates the brain and encourages memory.

SQ3R

(SQ3R stands for Survey, Question, Read, Recite, Review)

This system of practising retrieving things you have memorized is a tried and tested method based on the fact that for something to stay in long-term memory we need to revisit it – not regularly but at lengthening intervals. So we look at something today, memorize it by getting someone to ask us questions and check our answers, repeat it several times to be sure, then revisit it tomorrow. Later in the week we retrieve it again, then again once next week, and once next month. It is now firmly lodged in our memories.

A similar system is used for learning spellings. Look, Cover, Write and Check is a four-part process which follows the pattern of SQ3R. Teaching it to pupils, I emphasized it with hand gestures: Look (palms up and to the side), Cover (palms turn down to cover imaginary page), Write (use one hand to imitate writing) and Check (open palms up again).

Memories are capable of training with a little practice. School seems the best time to start.

Extending your vocabulary

Regular reading is the very best way to extend vocabulary. Reading just a little ahead of your ability means you come across vocabulary and other language structures which challenge, but with exposure become part of your active as well as your passive vocabulary. This applies to adults as well as teachers!

Pupils

- Make a note of new and unfamiliar words. New concepts often require new words and you can best understand them by adding them to a glossary or phrase book of your own.
- Organize the words in groups – words relating to the house, to the farm, food words, etc.
- Learn the words from one group at a time.
- Relate the words to a picture in your head of the place where they belong. Build up a picture of the farm with a farm house, barn, cowshed, piggery, etc., or a kitchen with table, chairs, cooker, window. Replay in your head a tour of each place while recalling the words.

Teachers

- Provide a glossary and add to it regularly as new concepts are taught.
- Help pupils to group words by theme or topic and supply pictures and descriptions.

A study skills chart

An example could be given, with the suggestion that pupils create their own posters, charts or advice booklets. It can be useful for parents as well as pupils, so produce it at a parents' evening. Parents usually want to help with something tangible like study and revision.

How to Begin

- Get Organized!
- Plan Ahead!
- Build a Timetable!
- Build in Leisure Time!
- Create Targets!
- Identify Objectives!
- Make Targets achievable!
- Give Rewards for Targets Achieved

Pace, Emotion

- Slow and Steady wins the race
- Go For It!
- Aim High – that's what stars are for!
- Shout, Don't Cry!
- If a Wall is too high, work your way around it

Note taking

- Use graphic organizers (coloured pens, bullets, under-lines, charts, drawings and diagrams)
- Make notes – succinct, clear, the nitty gritty
- Organize notes into meaningful chunks

Reflection

- Ask for help – from tutors and fellow students
- Ask questions – the only silly question is the one you don't ask
- Ask yourself – could I do this better? If so, how?

Study Environment

- Do study work in a convenient place
- Establish a routine
- Create a work station
- Use a calendar, a diary, a notebook or folder

Routine

- Start early – but it's never too late to begin!
- Do 5 minutes revision before bed
- Prioritize
- Balance work and play
- Foundations support building
- Stick to deadlines – it gets easier!

- Find the course summary or the syllabus. Write down the topic titles you've covered as headings on separate sheets of paper and leave a space below for your notes.
- Read a bit. Ask yourself what it means. Summarize what it means. Write that down. Move on to the next bit and read some more.

- Use a book or a handout that covers these topics. Deal with one topic at a time. Start to realize you *do* know something about this after all ...
- Get hold of likely exam questions. Find out what are the most important issues.
- Find answers to these and summarize the answers.
- Write notes on your notes, making them more concise every time.
- Memorize by look – cover – write – check. Then repeat.
- There – you *do* know something!

6

OTHER
APPROACHES TO
LEARNING

Teaching and learning styles

There are many theories or frameworks of learning:

Learning by doing (Piaget, Papart)
Learning in the company of others (Wenger)
Learning though dialogue (Vygotsky, Mercer)
Learning through reflection (Dewey, Jarvis)

Which one is your preferred learning style?

A learning style is a method or preferred strategy a pupil uses for acquiring knowledge. It's not *what* you learn but *how* you learn it.

Because pupils learn in different ways and at different speeds it makes sense to take into account the way they learn best. If we don't ask 'are you clever', but we ask 'how are you clever' we can show that we appreciate their preferred learning style and realize it may be better for them.

This doesn't mean that every child must be taught differently, and it doesn't mean that a child should always learn in the same style. In fact, quite the opposite – it's our job to show children a variety of learning styles and help them use different styles if they can be most effective. Pupils can be taught how to learn and if we provide them with a choice they will have the opportunity to choose what works best for them on a given occasion.

How does that work in the classroom? When we set a task we can recognize it can be done in a variety of ways. The outcome can be achieved via different routes. So if we want our pupils to learn about life in the London Blitz we could go about it in a variety of ways to appeal to a variety of learners. Having identified some appropriate resources to ensure they can use these if required, we might give them some outline and background before setting five tasks.

> *You must base your answer on the facts of living in London in the 1940s*
>
> 1. Produce a wall-chart showing bombing raids and damage to London.
> 2. Research and read about London in the Blitz to answer the question 'What was it like to be a ten year old child in London in the Blitz?'
> 3. Build a model of a house and its air-raid shelter. Explain how a real shelter was built and how it was used.
> 4. Write a personal diary as a day in the life of a ten year old child in the London Blitz.
> 5. How would you cope in this situation, when you could come out of your shelter after a night raid to find your house was just a heap of rubble? Design a plan for your family to make sure you keep safe and have everything you need to survive. When you've finished, in a small group, recreate a night raid and film it with sound effects.

These five tasks will all involve learning about the Second World War but they will appeal to different learners. A feedback session at the end of the project will make sure everyone knows about what was learned in terms of content. It could also be an opportunity to comment on how pupils found the task and why they chose it. This will give some insight into their preferred learning styles.

Learning competencies and skills

Bloom's *Taxonomy* (1956) categorizes learning competences and skills into six groups and suggests question cues for each:

Knowledge (of dates, events, information, subject content)
list, define, tell, describe, identify, show, label, collect, examine, tabulate, quote, name, who, when, where

Comprehension (understanding and interpreting)
summarize, describe, interpret, contrast, predict, associate, distinguish, estimate, differentiate, discuss, extend

Application (problem-solving, using theories in new situations)
apply, demonstrate, calculate, complete, illustrate, show, solve, examine, modify, relate, change, classify, experiment, discover

Analysis (seeing patterns and organizing information)
analyse, separate, order, explain, connect, classify, arrange, divide, compare, select, explain, infer

Synthesis (joined-up thinking, using old ideas to create new ones)
combine, integrate, modify, rearrange, substitute, plan, create, design, invent, what if?, compose, formulate, prepare, general-ize, rewrite

Evaluation (discriminate between ideas, assess the value of different presentations)
assess, decide, rank, grade, test, measure, recommend, convince, select, judge, explain, discriminate, support, conclude, compare, summarize

Bloom's Taxonomy has formed the basis of several developments in learning styles and information literacy. It succeeds in identifying different kinds of learning, different processes and different ways we can reach these by questioning our pupils.

It suggests ways of tapping into pupil skills and shows that memorizing traditional subject knowledge is not the only kind of learning.

Here is a taxonomy of learning styles – based on the work of Kathleen Butler (1987).

- Are your own *favoured* and *least liked* styles featured here?
- Do you love or loathe touchy-feely INSET sessions?
- Are you happier taking part or sitting quietly at the back?
- If you have to feed back after a training session do you prefer to talk, demonstrate, act out or to write a report?

- Which of the five tasks above (page 96) would you be happiest carrying out?

If you have your own preferences, remember pupils will too!

Kathleen Butler – Learning Styles

Variety	As organizers & thinkers	Needs as learners
REALISTIC	Linear, look for efficiency; Information-based, objective Tendency: to file it	Linear directions, specific assignments, charts data and tools, orderly, practical, structured, graphic methods
ANALYTICAL	Linear, look for the total picture; Logical, conceptual, knowledge-orientated, sceptical, goal-focused Tendency: to find a system	Intellectual dialogue, research topics, books, references, space to work alone, conceptual methods, reading, analysis
PRAGMATIC	Flexible structures; Practical, get the job done, improvising, on the spot action Tendency: to use what works	Real problems, hands-on experience, team players, action methods
PERSONAL	Holistic, look for immersion, intensity; People and process, harmony, connections, cooperation, conscientious	Collaborative learning, harmony, time to work things through, personal interpretation, arts, music writing

	Tendency: to make piles	
DIVERGENT	Holistic, look for variety, change; Discovery, investigation, ask what if, experimentation, challenge, risk, get on with it Tendency: to create chunks	Excitement, fast-paced exploration, freedom of choice, original problem-solving, unconventional methods

The five tasks about the London Blitz could fit the five learning styles above, though each one could also appeal to more than one style. Think about a group of pupils you know well. Where would each of them fit into Butler's five groups? Who is the efficient, objective and tidy child; who works best cooperating with people, working with them and encouraging them? What will happen if you put children with different styles together? Will they help each other because they have different skills, or will they conflict because they are too different? Will they understand each other because they are so similar in outlook or will they conflict because they are too much the same?

Try the same exercise with the group member types described by Belbin, below (pages 105–6).

The seven intelligences

The Kathleen Butler list is only one way of cutting the cake. In a series of publications Howard Gardner (1983) proposed a Theory of Multiple Intelligences in which he expanded the concept of intelligence to include such areas as music, spatial relations and interpersonal knowledge in addition to mathematical and linguistic ability.

He argued that 'reason, intelligence, logic, knowledge are not synonymous' and he formulated a list of seven intelligences:

Logical–mathematical

Detecting patterns, reasoning deductively and thinking logically. They like games and they follow rules. They enjoy processes, experiments and calculations. They are future scientists, accountants and lawyers.

Linguistic

Having skills in language, to express yourself linguistically and to remember information by using language. They express themselves through speech and writing. They may become authors, journalists, presenters or lecturers.

Spatial

Being able to solve problems by using mental images. They are visual, they doodle, use colour, like graphical balance. They work in diagrams, charts and maps and may be future architects, pilots and artists.

Musical intelligence

Recognizing and composing musical pitch, tone and rhythm. These pupils hum, sing, responding to both rhythm and melody. They enjoy multimedia topics and may become singers, instrumentalists or recording engineers.

Bodily-kinaesthetic

Using your mental abilities to coordinate your body movements. These pupils can't sit still; they relate to the world through their hands; they like role play, touching things, movement. They may become dancers, athletes or craftsmen.

Personal

Appreciating *interpersonal* feelings and intentions of others or having *intrapersonal* intelligence – the ability to understand your own feelings and motivations. *Intrapersonal* pupils may be shy, independent and reflective – future psychologists, novelists or programmers. They like independent projects and research. *Interpersonal* pupils are sociable, helpers, team players and enjoy interaction. They get involved in team sports and group work and may go on to become counsellors, politicians, teachers or entertainers.

Implications for classroom teachers

What do Gardner's Theory of Multiple Intelligences and Butler's categories of learning styles mean for classroom teachers?

The theory suggests that all seven intelligences (Logical–Mathematical, Linguistic, Spatial, Musical, Bodily-Kinesthetic, Interpersonal, Intrapersonal) are needed to function effectively in society. So teachers should treat all intelligences with equal importance – in contrast to the traditional education view, which emphasizes verbal and mathematical intelligences.

We can and should consider a broader range of talents and skills.

Another implication is that we should structure our presentation in a style which engages these intelligences. For example, when teaching about the Blitz, we might show maps, read poems, play contemporary popular music, organize a role play of an air raid, and read *The Exeter Blitz* and show extracts from the films, *The Machine Gunners* and *Goodnight, Mr Tom*. In this way we stimulate a wide variety of intelligences.

When we set a task or activity, we could offer variety, giving some pupils a free choice and encouraging others to make particular choices so they can develop extra skills. We could explain to the children what we are doing and how it will help them. We can encourage them to see that there's more than one way to skin a cat.

We could broaden our range of assessment, too, to incorporate the intelligences and learning styles we've encouraged. We might give credit for musicality, personal relations, physical adeptness and creativity as well as spelling and numeracy.

We could even create an 'intelligence profile' for each pupil and aim to develop the aspects of the profile which are weakest. For the child this helps their menu of skills; for us it gives a wider view on which to assess progress and encourage development. Assessing a broader range of learning skills is inclusive and encourages successful participation in the classroom. It helps pupils appreciate the strengths of team members too.

For similar reasons, consider using a *pupil portfolio* in which pupils can place a variety of material in different forms to demonstrate what they have achieved. This works well as an electronic portfolio too with hyperlinks to a range of sources. How to do this in practice is explained in Chapter 9. These are collections of best creative work which could include personal journals, and video recordings of activities.

It also helps to arrange groups thoughtfully. Generally primary school teachers can choose appropriate groups because they know their pupils' strengths and weaknesses in a variety of circumstances, but secondary school teachers see more pupils for less time and may have less information to go on. Friendship groups can help pupils be supportive of each other, but they can also distract from the task in hand.

It is a good idea sometimes to shake up groups and introduce variety. Deciding groups on the basis of a wide range of skills and learning styles and encouraging team members to work together and make best use of their specialisms is an excellent lesson for life and should result in more effective learning.

A quick way to create a learning styles' profile is to take one of several online tests. The results below show in both graphical and numeric form a deliberately distorted profile of Dave the Lonely Diarist. This would be useful starting point for a discussion with pupils on how to extend Dave's skills, leading on to their own personal range of skills. Armed with their unique chart they could quiz other pupils about how they work, learn, revise or study.

The 'Memletic' learning styles' inventory involves answering 50 questions about your learning preferences, e.g.

You like to listen. People like to talk to you
You like listening to music at work and in the car
You like to set budgets and other numerical goals
You use lots of hand gestures
Your favourite subject at school was English
You have a wide vocabulary

Learning Styles Inventory - Results Page

This page displays the results of your learning styles inventory. You can also select options below to compare your styles to other users of the site.

Page Mode: ˙ Normal ˙ Full screen (for printing) Refresh

Your results

These are the results of your inventory. The scores are out of 20 for each style. A score of 20 indicates you use that style often.

Style Scores

Style	Score
Visual	10
Aural	10
Verbal	15
Physical	2
Logical	4
Social	2
Solitary	16

Memletic Styles Graph:

Legend:
■ Your Style

More Options

Edit questions and answers
Edit/update your profile
Share your results
User Menu
Buy Report

from http://www.learning-styles-online.com/inventory/

You prefer to talk over problems with others
You keep a journal or personal diary

This is a psychometric test – a standard way of assessing particular aspects of human behaviour, both abilities and aspects of personality. They measure how you tend to react to particular situations, your motivation, values, attitudes and interests.

They can be very effective in revealing skills and traits which conventional examinations do not test, but they are better as a diagnostic tool than as a labelling machine. If the test shows that your strengths lie in solitary and verbal activities as in the diagram above, that could be a spur to encourage social and physical activities rather than a permanent sign that you will always be a solitary writer. These tests should be treated as a snapshot rather than a permanent label. If we can use such tests to recognize and develop strengths we can help pupils to become lifelong learners.

If you are considering a change of career you might find a psychometric test useful in identifying your strengths and preferences. A well-designed test will include check questions to reduce the possibility of the test outcome being consciously influenced.

It certainly helped me when I was considering moving out of the classroom into another career. A test acted as a dispassionate but observant friend – who in fact confirmed what friends and family had been observing for years!

Working together as part of a team

Coordination of individual strengths can create a whole team which is stronger than the separate parts. A teacher can create this in a class or a form, or can create subgroups within a class which work together or compete.

Working as a member of a team is a highly valued skill. The work of Dr Meredith Belbin (2003) shows the characteristics of successful teams and it can help if pupils recognize the team role they are best equipped to fulfil. People don't always take on the same role; a flexible member can take on more than one role and therefore potentially be a more valuable team member. Generally, however, most people prefer one of the following three categories:

- action-orientated
- people-orientated
- cerebral

Placing all the action-orientated pupils together could provide sparky activity while mixing them in with cerebral pupils might make the quiet child uncomfortable. However, creating a mixture of strengths is a good idea and pupils can learn from each other and achieve things collectively which they could not do on their own.

Belbin's team roles
(showing their Contributions and 'Allowable Weaknesses')

Plant
✓ Creative, imaginative, unorthodox. Solves difficult problems.

✗ Ignores incidentals. Too preoccupied to communicate effectively.

Coordinator
✓ Mature, confident, a good chairperson. Clarifies goals, promotes decision-making, delegates well.

✗ Can be seen as manipulative. Offloads personal work.

Monitor, evaluator
✓ Sober, strategic and discerning. Sees all options. Judges accurately.

✗ Lacks drive and ability to inspire others.

Implementer
✓ Disciplined, reliable, conservative and efficient. Turns ideas into practical actions.

✗ Rather inflexible. Slow to respond to new possibilities.

Completer, finisher
✓ Painstaking, conscientious, anxious. Searches out errors and omissions. Delivers on time.

✗ Tends to worry. Reluctant to delegate.

Resource investigator
✓ Extrovert, enthusiastic, communicative. Explores opportunities, develops contacts.

✗ Over-optimistic. Loses interest after initial enthusiasm.

Shaper
✓ Challenging, dynamic, thrives on pressure. Has the drive and courage to overcome obstacles.

✗ Tends to provoke. Offends people's feelings.

Teamworker
- ✓ Cooperative, mild, perceptive and diplomatic. Listens, builds, avoids friction.
- ✗ Indecisive in problem situations.

Specialist
- ✓ Single-minded, self-starting, dedicated. Provides rare knowledge and skills.
- ✗ Contributes in a limited field. Concentrates on technicalities.

Good team activities using the strengths of team members together include almost any series of mixed activities which use the strengths of individuals supported by the team as a whole. Members of Scout and Guide groups, Cadet Force, Duke of Edinburgh Award Scheme, etc. will probably do well at these activities. Armed Forces, Operation Raleigh and Management Teams develop the same idea.

The team must agree, which involves negotiation, problem-solving, socializing skills, common targets and the opportunity for many people to achieve. 'Rigging' the activities so the same individuals don't always win is not just fair play but positively educational – so if a low-achieving pupil has a known interest in dinosaurs, make sure his expertise can be used!

- Organizing an event (sports day, garden fête, fun day for the family)
- Newspaper Day (collapse the timetable, gather news and articles, write and design a newspaper or series of web pages by the end of the school day)
- Orienteering Team Challenge (with running, swimming and cycling events, map-reading and puzzle challenges)
- Camping expeditions (with targets for distance, cooking, navigation and other task completions)
- Quests and Treasure Hunts
- Moving the team and its equipment over a 'stream' using rope and milk crates

Thinking skills

Steve Higgins, *et al.* (2005) from the University of Newcastle have classified Thinking Skills into three broad categories:

- philosophical
- brain-based learning
- cognitive intervention

Philosophical approaches

Here there is an emphasis on questioning and reasoning, particularly by a class. The teacher identifies an issue to be discussed by the whole group then facilitates the discussion and the class's reasoning processes.

Brain-based learning

Recent research into the working of the human brain has informed the writing of Edward de Bono and Eric Jensen. Accelerated Learning, Multiple Intelligences (Gardner 1983) and research into learning styles all use brain research as a springboard for creating classroom activities. De Bono's book *Six Thinking Hats* (1987) refers to his CoRT (Cognitive Research Trust) programme.

Cognitive intervention

It is generally agreed that thinking skills techniques need to be integrated into learning rather than taught as entirely separate skills, if they are to be properly absorbed by the learner and seen as relevant to their learning.

A programme called *Instrumental Enrichment* by Reuven Feuerstein in the 1950s consisted of specially designed activities designed to improve learners' cognitive functioning (Feuerstein *et al.* 1980). The theories of Vygotsky and of Piaget have also been applied to try and improve effective learning through specifically taught activities.

Reynolds and Muijs (2001) identify three main methods for teaching higher-order learning skills, which will provide problem-solving strategies for learners. It is assumed that the problems which the learners are posed will be sufficiently challenging to transform their ways of thinking and approaching problems, but also sufficiently meaningful that they can relate to them in a practical way.

Heuristic
(Breaking up the problem into its constituent parts)

Understanding the problem
Sorting out what's relevant and what isn't. Teachers can offer a wide range of examples and help pupils to recognize typical types; have them explain the problem to others; look at the problem from creative and unconventional viewpoints.

Selecting or planning the solution
Decide on an appropriate solution.

Breaking the problem into smaller chunks, they might work backwards from the goal towards the problem.

Teachers might ask pupils to explain and justify each step as they reach it or pass it.

Executing the plan

Evaluating the result
Does the answer make sense? In a mathematical problem the ability to estimate should show if the decimal point is in the right place. In a practical problem a sketch or some other visualization may provide proof. Often another pupil can spot what the problem-solvers were too close to see clearly.

Metacognitive

If we are aware of our own thinking and can look critically at our own problem-solving techniques, we are better armed to be effective thinkers. If we can ask why we are doing something and how this might solve the problem, we can think more purposefully and reflect on our thinking instead of just letting it happen to us.

There are a number of techniques for teaching metacognitive skills:

- Explain why problem-solving strategies are important. Watch other pupils or adults in cooperative problem-solving to see other people using both effective and ineffective strategies.
- Work problems through diagrammatically in front of the class. Show the whole-problem resolution, which includes dead ends and decisions not to explore further as well as the neat solution.
- Have the whole class work on a problem with teacher as moderator. Let pupils experiment with a variety of strategies and try new ideas until the right solution has been found. Then evaluate and review the strategies.
- Use 'scaffolding cards' printed with basic prompt questions. When working in small groups questions such as 'What am I doing now?' 'What else could I be doing instead?' will help pupils internalize their metacognitive thinking.

Cognitive acceleration in science and maths

Thinking skills can be taught in a subject-based rather than a general way. The Cognitive Acceleration in Science Education (CASE) project delivers thinking skills in a structured way with five main elements. These are common to all subjects:

1. Pupils learn essential vocabulary and clarify the problem.
2. They are then presented with something which seems to contradict their previous knowledge or understanding.
3. Next they experience an activity which extends their current levels of understanding and skills. The teacher helps help them build up higher-level reasoning patterns.
4. Pupils review and reflect on their problem-solving.
5. The new skills or knowledge are applied to different contexts.

McGuinness (1998)

Active learning

The Learning Research and Development Centre (1991) lists the following higher-order thinking skills:

- Size up and define a problem that isn't neatly packaged.
- Determine which facts and formulas stored in memory might be helpful for solving a problem.
- Recognize when more information is needed, and where and how to look for it.
- Deal with uncertainty by 'brainstorming' possible ideas or solutions when the way to proceed isn't apparent.
- Carry out complex analyses or tasks that require planning, management, monitoring, and adjustment.
- Exercise judgement in situations where there aren't clear-cut 'right' and 'wrong' answers, but more and less useful ways of doing things.
- Step outside the routine to deal with an unexpected breakdown or opportunity.

Clearly these strategies are designed for coping with the unexpected, with problems which are not routine. This is difficult but important to teach. It is real learning. One way of expressing this is that you are seeking to 'expand the consciousness' of the child.

You can encourage pupils to apply what they learn in one curriculum area to another. This kind of 'joined-up curriculum thinking' becomes rather rare in secondary schools, though a primary school class teacher with a single class should find it comes naturally. We can all help pupils to develop enquiry skills using real (rather than artificial) situations. You can provide opportunities for predicting and making a hypothesis, which is then tested by enquiry and the results reflected upon.

These are not cut-and-dried exercises. There is every reason for you the teacher not to know the answer before the enquiry begins. If pupils try to deduce from evidence they have collected themselves, try to estimate results before they accurately calculate them, try to check and monitor them and their progress, judge and value what they have found – they are taking part in a genuine learning activity and challenging themselves. If these skills are developed in activities where they suffuse the whole curriculum, rather than being artificially taught in isolation, there is every reason to believe that they will enhance learning throughout the school.

There are many sources of detailed information about active learning and associated thinking skills and several are referred to in the bibliography. The terminology for the many schemes is varied, but look out for

Critical Thinking
Philosophy for Children
The Brain Gym
Accelerated Learning
Creative Thinking
Logical Reasoning Skills
Six Thinking Hats

The last is by Edward de Bono (1987) whose idea of 'lateral thinking' has been influential in many areas. *Six Thinking Hats* describes a technique of applying different kinds of thinking to different situations.

Active learning study

'Active' here is the opposite of passive, to reinforce the idea that learning is not 'filling up the little pitchers with knowledge' as Gradgrind (Dickens's *Hard Times*) has it, but actually doing something to embed learning into an active mind. Study revision and classroom learning are at their least effective when a teacher sprays words at a somnolent class.

Inactive	Active
Don't think	Prepare questions to ask
Treat lessons as isolated incidents	Undertake advance reading
Listen without thinking	Set yourself questions about what you are being told
Turn up and tune out	Ask questions when given the opportunity
Just write things down	Make methodical and selective notes using graphical organizers, headings, etc.
Copy out neatly	Rework the notes soon after a lecture or reading and link ideas and information
Believe that learning happens only in classrooms	Review notes at intervals and add newly learned key points where appropriate
Copy directly from notes into an essay	Discuss ideas with others
Treat lessons as interruptions to the rest of life	Mull things over and form a personal view
Leave handouts and notes, if any, untouched from day to day	Organize information
Treat editing and rewriting as an unnecessary chore	Draft and redraft your writing
When the last word is written, it's over	Evaluate your own work
Treat positive criticism in a negative to way	Use feedback constructively improve future work

- If revising, don't leave until the last minute. Read and think about notes continuously throughout the duration of the course.
- Summarize a group of notes in a single sentence.
- Use graphical device and organizers such as highlighters, icons, pictures, colours, spidergrams, mind maps, charts, diagrams, etc.

- Think of real-life examples.
- List ideas or examples and rank them in order of importance.
- Write questions about the topic using who, why, what, where, when and how – then try to answer them. Research any questions you can't answer.
- Write action plans, with dates – and try to keep to them.
- Teach what you've learned to someone else.
- Keep a reflective journal.
- Identify the main points and the most convincing points.
- Note the best part of a book; the best paragraph.
- Invent essay titles and prepare ten-minute essay outlines to answer them.
- List key points.
- Discuss and debate with others. Argue your case but also listen to what they say.

Gender

One highly significant feature of learning is the influence of our gender. Women have a more substantial connecting cord between the left and right sides of the brain and more cones in the eye retina. So they can multi-task and have a wider range of vision, while men have vision focused on distance. This apparently can be traced back to primitive man's role as hunter, where the man's vision is more directed and focused, and the woman's role in the home where they must be more aware of dangers from the periphery.

Although it is not universally true that males are more aggressive than females, it is fairly common. Females on the other hand are more likely to negotiate and compromise. Research shows, on average, that females have more verbal ability than males, while males have better visual–spatial skills and tend to do better at abstract mathematics.

Learning strategies need to take these differences into account.

Helping boy underachievers
An Ofsted study in 2003, *Boys Achievement in Secondary Schools*,

studied three types of interventions that were followed by improvements in learning.

- teaching single-sex classes or groups at secondary level
- mentoring and role-modelling by adults, including teachers within the school, and other pupils, at secondary level
- additional literacy support from adult volunteers from outside school at primary level

In many of the schools, the key to improving boys' performance lay in improving boys' attitudes. As one head teacher said: 'We wanted to overcome the culture that states they cannot be seen to be successful without losing their street cred.'

Noble and Bradford (2000) provide an example of an English teacher's approach to teaching *Macbeth* to Year 11 boys. The teacher began by giving pupils a questionnaire about their preferred learning style, which she then used to help her choose appropriate teaching styles, which included:

- presenting some of the text in tabulated form
- using statistics and graphs
- breaking *Macbeth* into recurring sections of horror, humour, fantasy and action
- setting short, written tasks, often in the form of games or quizzes
- setting small-group work to produce verbal accounts of the story
- using only a small amount of video to illustrate key points
- using ICT to proofread, edit and display
- raising the status of oral work and introducing a reward system

The most common pattern for a mentoring session was a 15 to 30 minute session, usually out of lesson, with a member of staff mentoring an individual pupil. Typical issues for discussion included:

- planning of homework and coursework tasks
- time management and meeting deadlines
- monitoring and using the pupils' assessment data
- presentation of work
- liaison with parents about pupils' progress
- careers planning
- revision techniques

A case study quoted by the NFER study focused on 22 boys in Year 10 who had been taught science in low-ability single-sex groups. The authors identified a range of factors that teachers had to consider in teaching such groups. These included:

- listening to boys to make them feel valued and respected
- identifying boys who are under pressure and providing them with pastoral support
- helping boys to develop and clarify their career ambitions
- helping boys to organize their work more effectively
- developing tasks which require thinking rather than copying
- using examples which are relevant to the boys' lives
- using humour

The authors concluded:

> The research highlighted the importance of teachers taking the time to listen to the boys as a means of establishing good relationships with them. The boys appreciated teachers who showed that they cared about them and wanted to teach them. It made them feel valued as learners and individuals.

Alternative schools

The National Curriculum, meeting the requirements of the *Education Act* of 1996, provides a National Framework, provides (some would say imposes) a framework on state-controlled schools

> to enable all schools to respond effectively to national and local priorities, to meet the individual learning needs of all pupils and

to develop a distinctive character and ethos rooted in their local communities.

(DfES 1999)

Alternative schools, by definition, provide something different from the state-centred schools which have to conform to an approved centralist curriculum. Often they emphasize the role they have in developing the needs of the individual. Some include boarding facilities. Although inspected by Ofsted to ensure certain minimum standards they range from home-tutored individual pupils to historic private schools, and from specialist schools centred on a single elite skill to philosophically liberal schools initiated by a single educationalist.

However strongly we support a system of schools provided by the state and which is obliged to cater for everyone, we would be unwise to imagine it is the only – or even the best – way to organize education. Both state and private sectors have a great deal to learn from each other and neither has a monopoly on effective learning. The most successful school is not necessarily right for all pupils.

If we look beyond the buildings and the environment of the school, and its stated curriculum we can sense its relative formality or informality – its overall ethos. Difficult to pin down, describe or publish, the school's ethos may be what makes us choose it as a place to learn or a place to work. Vulnerable to the froth of advertising language if described in the school brochure or website, it may nevertheless include how the school develops a sense of motivation and curiosity in learning, whether it emphasizes competition or cooperation, whether it instils a sense of self-esteem and whether all these are achieved by a system of incentives and rewards. Do the pupils feel they can succeed? Are they able to cope with some failure? Are they given opportunities to succeed? How are they encouraged to succeed meaningfully and without vacuous praise?

Steiner schools

Steiner schools are based on the philosophy of Rudolph Steiner, who founded his first school in Germany in 1919. There are now nearly 900 around the world. They stand for:

- Human values in learning communities
- Respecting the integrity of the child
- Developing healthy intellect and creative potential

The Steiner Waldorf Schools Fellowship claims:

> Steiner schools have their own comprehensive and distinctive curriculum and teaching method for pupils up to 18. This curriculum is based on a pedagogical philosophy that places emphasis on the whole development of the child, including a child's spiritual, physical and moral well-being as well as academic progress. There is a strong emphasis on social abilities and the development of pre-numeracy and literacy skills. Formal learning begins later, and learning is done in a very creative and artistic environment.

Hands-on learning takes place through activities such as gardening as well as conventional classroom lessons.

The schools teach foreign languages from an early age and offer a broad curriculum which includes science and humanities throughout, and music and movement are integrated with learning across the curriculum. It is a holistic system with an emphasis on educating rounded individuals and without the regular testing of the state system.

Montessori schools

These follow the philosophy of Maria Montessori (1870–1952)
   The specific elements of Montessori education include:

- Children are grouped in mixed ages and abilities, with a 3–6-year span.
- Children are always free to move around the room instead of staying at desks.
- There are no grades, or other forms of reward or punishment, subtle or overt.

- Children can work on any material they understand at any time. They move on when they are ready.
- Teachers are trained to teach one child at a time, and to oversee thirty or more children working on a wide variety of self-chosen work.
- At any one time in a class all subjects (maths, language, science, history, geography, art, music, etc.) will be being studied, at all levels.
- Adults and children do not interrupt someone who is busy at a task.
- Education of movement and of character come before education of the mind, children learning to take care of themselves, their environment, each other – cooking, cleaning, building, gardening, being considerate and helpful.
- There are no curriculum requirements except those set by the state for specific grades. Most of the time the children develop, with less and less adult direction as they grow older, individual paths of research and learning, individually and in groups.
- The Montessori teacher spends a lot of time during teacher training practising the many lessons with materials in all areas – maths, language, science, history, geography, art, music. The teacher learns to recognize a child's readiness for a specific lesson, and guides individual progress.
- All subjects are interwoven with each other, not taught in isolation, the teacher teaching the researching of all subjects.
- All kinds of intelligences and styles of learning are nurtured.
- The test of whether or not the system is working lies in the behaviour of the children, their happiness, and love of learning and work.

Edited from Stephenson (2000)

Home schooling

Keeping a child at home, either by choice or because of illness, is generally seen as disadvantageous in terms of socialization, though it may be a distinct advantage in terms of individual bespoke learning. With a parent as the main tutor, additional tutors can be brought in for specific purposes if required to give curriculum breadth, but it remains a middle-class choice because of the need for the parents to be educated themselves. The relationship is likely to be intense and can produce difficulties at adolescence when the child seeks to become more independent. For this reason alone home schooling often stops at the end of the primary phase. Socializing with peers can be difficult as children develop adult social skills which set them apart from other children of the same age. However, taking part in local sports or music groups, the Scouting movement or arts and crafts groups should provide adequate socializing opportunities.

Various case studies have shown high achievers who have come from home schooling, though cause and effect can be hard to disentangle. Advocates of home schooling sometimes argue that traditional schools are no better than factories generating, at best, conventional citizens. As a correspondent to *The Times* (6 August 2004) put it:

> Compulsory mass state schooling nurtures conformity and homogeny, low self-esteem, bullying and poor socialization amid learners who are disaffected with learning. They give up on anything creative if the bell has decreed playtime, and they ask permission to eat, speak and play for 11 years.

This rather extreme attitude nevertheless may be a response to those schools where gifted and talented or unconventional pupils are not provided with suitable opportunities for personal learning or scope to work at their own pace. Why do we make extensive provision for less-able pupils, but relatively little for the gifted and talented? Is it because the less able are generally more troublesome?

Personalized learning

I once went for interview as an aspiring young English teacher and was told that the department was 'an examination machine' and I shouldn't take the job if I didn't like that. I didn't, so I left. But it made me think. At the time I was teaching in an extremely flexible environment – a series of interconnected classrooms teaching the same class of 'RoSLA' (Raising of the School Leaving Age) kids for 9 hours or more a week. When they decided to raise the school leaving age resource materials were produced which recognized that pupils who had been due to leave school at 15 might feel thwarted and take it out on the school unless they were given some practical, useful and interesting things to do. I taught English and Social Studies CSE Mode 3 courses.

Mode 3 was essentially a course you constructed in your own school or together with a couple of other schools; you constructed it, taught it, marked it and had your work moderated by a representative from the exam board. These were innovative times: we went on visits and trips, some residential, some projects based on the local community; we taught life skills from why democracy is important to how to open a bank account to avoiding unnecessary pregnancy. Sometimes we collapsed the timetable and taught in a team of four, sometimes we taught our own classes of 15–16 year olds in groups of 15 or so. I have rarely come to know pupils as well as I knew them. I suppose I have been struggling to regain that level of independence in my teaching ever since.

For those who learn differently, who find the conventional 'factory of learning' model demotivating, a personal learning plan could prevent them leaving the system altogether. However, we persist in shoehorning pupils of all shapes and sizes into standardized boxes – one-hour chunks of time which have no link or connection between them. It is astonishing that any pupil can get through a day in which science follows English, then food technology, then PE and finally French. It's an incoherent ragbag where, even where there could be connections between topics, they are rarely made because each teacher is sealed into a department structure where sharing teaching ideas with other departments is anathema.

The secondary school timetable is constructed by organizational criteria, with a dash of tradition. Timetable success is defined by having all the boxes in the grid neatly filled – not by creating a coherent learning experience for each child.

Let us use our powerful technology to leap into a further dimension where individual learning plans can be created for our pupils and ultimately by our pupils. Where form tutors become 'learning tutors' consulting with parents and pupils and tracking progress with an efficient schools management system which deals with the learning experience as well as the more mundane absence and lateness. Such a system could be the point where educating the individual takes over from mass schooling and where different routes to common goals don't compromise high standards.

Charles Leadbeater (2005) warns:

> Personalised learning is not cafeteria-style learning: picking your own curriculum from a wider self-service menu. Personalised learning should equip children to make choices about which subjects to study, what settings to study in, what styles of learning to employ. But choice is just a means to turn children into more engaged and motivated investors in their own education. The main goal is to encourage higher aspirations.

The interaction between pupil and teacher is vital but can be extended to include peer mentoring and collaboration across schools and with the community. As the African proverb has it: 'It takes a village to raise a child'. Learning is an innate drive, but children learn at different speeds and in different ways, with different ambitions and interests. The Victorian one-size-fits-all model may work for the academic and the biddable but it is bound to fail the unconventional and the disillusioned. Collaborative environments enabled by vision and technology can create opportunities for enhanced personal learning. This might even see the decline of the huge comprehensive school, originally gathered together in crowds of 2,000 or so to save money, but which could become more personal and human in scale with 500 or so children in a system where staff and pupils know and support each other, collaborating with other similar-sized schools as required by using video conferencing, online polling and shared resources and expertise.

The notion of differentiation has been taken up enthusiasti-cally in some quarters, but it is only by unbinding the restrictive curriculum and its rigid brick walls that real differentiation can be reached. A school is becoming one of the few large organizations where its members arrive and leave at rigidly fixed times. This need not be so. You may think this is airy-fairy and impractical, but it need not be so. Visit the DfES Innovation Unit and you'll see they're already thinking about it!

Teaching methods

Throughout this book I've emphasized learning at the expense, perhaps, of teaching. This is quite deliberate because I think we need to focus on learning more than any other single thing – it is the whole point of education. Also if learning works, then teaching must be working too. But I'd like briefly to look at some general teaching methods which we may take for granted but which deserve a revisit.

Think of this as a list of options you can use to teach anything. Sometimes one will be quickest and easiest, sometimes another. Sometimes one will be slower to have an effect in the short term but will be more likely to endure.

Instruction
Very straightforward, this. By telling pupils something, they may not remember it, let alone learn it. However some things do need to be told and accepted without question. Telling a pupil that they must not throw a javelin until the arena is clear is important and unarguable. Health and safety may need reinforcement and could be helped by scary pictures of injured pupils. Direct instruction still has its place. Lectures are considered an acceptably efficient means of conveying information, though note-taking enhances effective learning and tasks set to consolidate and test learning are usually necessary.

The 4-Mat system developed by Bernice McCarthy in 1979 (1981), is described as 'a cycle for delivering instruction' though here 'instruction' is the broader meaning of educating and covers key stages in gaining attention, encouraging pupils to think about a topic, then practise and develop it. These are core elements of learning and although the 4-Mat system goes into far greater depth, its basic eight steps are:

1. Connect
2. Attend
3. Imagine
4. Inform
5. Practise
6. Extend
7. Refine
8. Perform

Example

Giving an example which fits in with the pupil's own experience makes an idea relevant. If they can't relate to it they will have difficulty understanding. So we use the phrase 'like this' and show a picture, an object, a movement. 'Here's one I prepared earlier' is an example; so is 'Do this like me' and giving a demonstration. We should also remember that our whole attitude – caring, helping, being patient, or being bad-tempered, harsh and intolerant – will have a considerable effect on our pupils. Long after they have forgotten the details of the Civil War they will remember their patient and long-suffering teacher.

Analogy or comparison

This is similar to 'example' above but uses simile and metaphor to describe things and to connect them to the pupil's experience. Describing the way that if you bend back the spine of a paperback book, the pages pop up 'like bread from a toaster' adds a vivid image to the lesson. Underlining the importance of knowledge about grammar by describing it as a set of tools in a box makes understanding prepositions or word classes more practical and less abstract. Making meaningful comparisons between historical figures or events and modern examples can bring history to life.

Experiment and discovery

Learning by doing is practical and creative. As I explain in Chapter 8, 'I hear and I forget, I see and I remember, I do and I understand.' Finding out by doing may take longer, but the learning lasts longer too. Not all experiments are carried out in a creative way, of course. Those chemistry 'experiments' I did as a child, adding one chemical to another in a test tube, did nothing to inspire me, and of course the same 'experiment' was carried out year after year with the same predictable results. However running around the school and measuring each others' lung capacity or making structures from simple materials and testing their maximum weight-bearing, are real experiments where the process is personal and lively and the result is not pre-ordained.

Collaboration and competition
Working with someone else or in a small team gives many benefits. The additional points of view and different ideas can inspire an individual and while working with others can also be a challenge, it is in itself a learning opportunity.

One team pitted against another can increase a challenge and lever up the level of achievement. Failure at one competitive task does not mean that the child is a failure; success is rarely achieved without risk and coping with failure is a valuable lesson (up to a point).

Computer-mediated learning
Using a computer need not be an exclusive or solitary activity. Using a computer as an additional tool to complement or supplement other learning can be far more effective. Computer suites are useful for intensive computer training, but computers sprinkled liberally around areas which are used for different kinds of work can lead to a more balanced and practical use. Computers are good at some things and are not so good at others, however there is a tendency for some pupils to think of them as the best and the only way to achieve something. They are valuable tools, but not the only ones.

Mentoring
Help and guidance comes not only from the teacher and teaching assistant but also from peers and older pupils who approach things from a different background. Older children listening to younger children reading aloud help not only the learner who deserves an audience, but themselves as they learn about

responsibility and caring. Peer-support groups countering bullying can be particularly effective. Naturally, teachers need not only to stand back from the learning process but to be at hand to support the mentor too.

Fitting into existing constructs

This has been mentioned in using analogy and comparison. Building on prior learning is an essential part of any kind of structured learning and will dictate the starting point and the speed at which future learning can take place. Here I'm using the word 'construct' as in the personal construct theory of Kelly (1955) where he proposes that our processes, thoughts and actions are psychologically channelled by the ways in which we anticipate events and that we differ from each other in how we construe events.

Frameworks

Quite formal frameworks can be used by teachers to structure responses and help build up complex skills. Using scaffolding, writing frames, supporting with prompts, we can offer an overall shape into which pupils can slot their personal answers, or provide part of a pattern to encourage pupils to create the rest. A framework could be a model, an incomplete shape or a template, for writing a formal letter, structuring an essay by providing paragraph headings, providing a set of questions needing individual answers which then combine to form a full response. A framework banishes the tyranny of the blank A4 page.

7

CREATIVITY AND
IMAGINATION

Another book in this series, *Letting the Buggers be Creative* by Sue Cowley (2005), deals with this area in greater depth, but creativity and imagination are so closely linked to learning that they deserve some space here too.

The National Curriculum itself does not abolish creativity or imagination, but many people observed that it did not emphasize creativity and failed to mention enjoyment.

Learning should be fun, stimulating, enjoyable. If learning is to be lifelong, then it has to be enjoyable and interesting enough for people to continue learning voluntarily throughout their lives. It usually is for younger children but as they move further on in the education system some of that fun and imagination seems to disappear.

Some lay the blame at the door of a prescriptive curriculum, some at the examination and assessment system which inevitably pushes schools into teaching to the test. Some say that it is adolescent hormones creating challenging teenagers whose teachers react by creating a more disciplined and structured environment. Behind all this lies the criticism of so-called 'trendy teaching methods' which are said not to teach 'the basics'. Perhaps this has led to teachers themselves downgrading their own creativity and imagination.

Whatever the reasons, there is clearly a need for learning to be stimulating. Learning can't always be fun. Some things require hard work if they are to be mastered, and the satisfaction when hard work produces worthwhile skills is all the deeper for the effort that has been put in. However, imagination and creativity are not at odds with learning basic skills; they can enhance them.

Creativity

Creativity does not feature in Gradgrind's education system. It takes time, so seems to be less efficient. It produces results which may not be be quantified or judged by conventional standards. Creativity is different, it doesn't fit in, it's off the wall, oddball, from left field.

All the more reason for encouraging it, I would say. Yet in an overcrowded curriculum led by targets, success is counted in conventional ways and bean counters don't know what to do with creativity.

And yet our society needs creative people. Our media rely upon them, our society may depend upon creative people to come up with solutions to problems which are not being solved by conventional means. The ability to 'think different' is prized by business.

Tim Brighouse has said that very young children should experience:

Looking after animals regularly
Taking part in nursery rhymes
Playing in groups at shops, fire stations and hospitals
Dressing up in groups
Caring for a younger child

Having seen young adolescents in hot-seating exercises and class debates performing better when wearing appropriate hats from a dressing-up box, I think it is not only the very young who gain from these experiences.

Teachers who are secure in their subject knowledge can be confident in developing creativity to help children achieve their potential, and that potential can in turn be measured through national benchmarks. In short, creativity can lead to the highest of standards, however they are measured.

Creative presentation of a topic by the teacher can lead to more effective learning. Sometimes teachers feel they are slacking by not working actively in front of a class. In fact, organizing activities so that pupils have more independence or so that their focus is on group work can move the focus from you at the front to you at the side, where you can help or guide when help is needed.

Many teachers feel they cannot afford the time for their pupils to learn more creatively because the bureaucracy of the National Curriculum urges them on to 'more efficient' ways of learning. The National Curriculum is such a weighty body of targets and programmes that in some cases it has become the cart controlling the horse.

The following analysis of the vocabulary frequency of National Curriculum Targets comes from *100 Essential Lists for Teachers* (Grey 2005b)

KS3 English
- Words which appear once:
  Whereby, world, wildlife, whom, weave, unconventional, thou, once, simulated, jokes, Goldilocks, correct, bus-stop, mathematics, grammar
- Words which don't appear at all:
  Stimulated, kids, enjoy, love, fun, excitement, lively, enthusiasm

KS3 Mathematics
- Words which appear once:
  arbitrarily, digit, gallons, isosceles, thinking, obeys, obtuse, obvious, odd, one-thousandths, SAS, stem-and-leaf, pie, pints
- Words which don't appear at all:
  enjoy, love, fun, excitement, lively, enthusiasm, imagination

KS3 Science
- Words which appear once:
  toxic, taxonomic, superglue, snowboards, questions, flowering, ear, deafness, cytoplasm, antagonistic, alcohol
- Words which don't appear at all:
  birth, creation, sex, enjoy, love, fun, excitement, lively, enthusiasm, imagination

I'm glad to say that imaginary, imaginative and imagined do appear several times in the English attainment targets. I also acknowledge that later initiatives have tried to reintroduce creative strands, but for a time at least the notion of learning for its pleasure, doing things for fun, was replaced by learning to the test, pursuing a bureaucratic paperchase and the tyranny of targets.

So, without compromising the National Curriculum as a useful framework and a checklist of topics which can be taught, how can we introduce a degree of spontaneity, of personal response, of imagination into learning?

Creative ideas

I hesitate to offer a list of creative ideas. After all, I've just criticized a national framework. I'm also acutely aware that by the very act of writing a list I am somehow starting to squeeze out the very imagination and spontaneous creativity I seek to encourage. But you have to start somewhere. If any of these ideas even sows a seed which leads on to your pupils appreciating and enjoying their learning then it's worthwhile.

The ideas below could be as usefully be taken up by teachers as by pupils. Knowing that teacher is reading or writing at the same time as the class demonstrates that it is not an isolated classroom act but a genuine life activity.

Creative writing

Write your own poetry as well as analysing it. One helps the other; appreciation of the work of others is enhanced by our understanding of the process and our own writing can benefit from an awareness of how others have gone about it. Creative writing takes many forms and has been unfairly dismissed. A teacher showing her own attempts of writing, including corrections and revisions, enhances the experience.

The above is equally true of art and drama. Reading and writing, performing and criticizing, creating and deconstructing are all creative acts.

Creating by using techniques which stimulate imagination is very useful in the classroom. Take a newspaper article and cut it into small pieces, then reassemble it as a poem. Take a description and recreate it as a poem with a shape appropriate to the topic (see Lewis Carroll and Apollinaire). Write stories stimulated by a random collection of objects or words. Combine random objects into a drama or a piece of sculpture. Making unusual connections between things and ideas is a great 'thinking skill'. Like seeing pictures in a piece of wood or a blazing fire, our minds are somehow set free to create unusual metaphors for a different world.

Invent new words

Can you create new words where none currently exist, or blend words together for new meanings?

> *volvocracy* – government by people who drive Volvos
> *pestiary* – directory of unpleasant people and animals (cf. bestiary)
> *abombination* – terrorist explosion
> *dripod* – waterproof cover for mp3 player
> *trypod* – competition to win an iPod
> *skypod* – wireless-enabled iPod
> *commissionary* – obsessive salesman
> *red pencilitis* – students' fear of having their work marked
> *carperpetuation* – the act, when vacuuming, of running over a string or a piece of lint many times without picking it up
> *telecrastination* – the act of letting the phone ring at least twice before you pick it up, even when you're only inches away.

Search for 'neologism' on the Internet, or read *The Meaning of Tingo* by Adam Jacot de Boinod (2005).

Invent new worlds

Science fiction can help as a stimulus, but the worlds of *The Lord of the Rings*, Harry Potter, Beatrix Potter, *The Wind in the Willows* and *The Borrowers* all describe worlds separate from ours where readers can retreat and imagine. That's not escapism, it's imagination.

Experiment

The most effective experiment is one where the result is not already known. In mathematics this may involve 'what if' scenarios using spreadsheets. In science it is surely more exciting to see what happens if you are not simply following the route taken by thousands of people before you.

A message from science is that a negative proof or result can be as valuable as a positive one. We learn as much, or sometimes more, when our bridge of toilet rolls and straws collapses as when it holds up. Might we learn more from a cake which collapses as one which rises? Might we learn more from a debate in which we fail to convince others, or a sculpture which fails to stand up?

Problem-solving

This need not be a problem which has a definite solution. A Su Doku puzzle or a Word Search have known solutions. However, the number of uses for a brick, or how we might best measure the volume of air in a car, require thought and the bouncing of ideas off each other. How we personally might reduce the problem of global warming will also be an information retrieval exercise, while how to persuade everyone to keep the school and grounds clean and tidy will involve everyone in thinking and looking for practical solutions. It might involve speaking and listening, reading and writing, drawing and designing, but it is also worthwhile on an imaginative level alone.

Set up situations where imagination is stimulated. Go out of the classroom and record your reactions using your five senses. Use background music and light shows while writing or painting. Play games of consequences where one person's contribution sparks off more ideas from another. Brainstorm in groups and solve real problems using limited materials.

Empathy

Empathy is a focused use of imagination. It is much discussed by historians who seek a balance between knowledge and appreciation by, for example, visiting the World War One battlefields and recording reactions in diaries. Enacting a Civil War battle on the school field is memorable and adds life to historical record. Carrying a fresh egg safely for a whole school day can instil a surprising sense of responsibility in otherwise reckless pupils.

Role play

If introduced sensitively, this allows people to leave behind their daily hangups and pretend to be someone else. A basic checklist of things to say for a debate, or essential viewpoints for this character are often helpful to move youngsters into role. Audience reaction will do the rest. A role for the audience, as recording clerks, witnesses, jurors or journalists can help maintain the atmosphere. Shy participants can sometimes be encouraged by having the audience behind them so they are less conscious of being watched.

Areas of unreality

Explore areas of unreality. What kind of counting system would we have if we had 12 fingers instead of 10? How would our built environment be different if our heads were below our bottoms? How would our houses be different if we had only one finger on each hand and no opposing thumbs? How could we communicate without speech? Read some really imaginative short science fiction stories such as *The Tunnel Under the World* (1954) by Frederick Pohl, or *Computers Don't Argue* (1965) by G. R. Dickson, or *The Ruum* (1953) by Arthur Porges. Watch imaginative films such as *Blade Runner* or *The Matrix* (choose atmosphere not horror or violence) and discuss possible futures. Talk about ancient myths and modern religious beliefs, possible futures after death, the existence of a deity.

Drawing/creating something substantial

While other classes drew simple pyramids and coloured them in, a colleague of mine had the children build a life-size camel in the classroom; terribly inconvenient – amazingly memorable. Ask to use temporary boarding around a building site for a class mural. Chalk a giant picture on the playground. Divide a small picture into a grid and enlarge it into large panels to become a giant ceiling picture. Build papier mâché planets and hang them around the school to show the relative sizes and distances

133

between them. Create a nature trail, a tunnel of multimedia experience for a museum, an orienteering route, a radio programme or a television broadcast.

Discovery learning

Discovery learning involves finding out by doing it yourself, and the prospect of failing is part of that. Where planning and rehearsal can almost eliminate the chance of failure, there is an alternative of pitching in with the minimum of practice and just following the flow. With only a very basic instruction in cameras and microphones an enthusiastic group can turn out a TV news broadcast in a morning. The secret is to have challenging deadlines so there is no time for scripts to be crafted and redrafted; the light is green and you're live!

Such improvisation, which is a technique much used in drama and in music to explore and express, calls upon imagination and pushes you to think on your feet and produce a reaction. The result is less important than the participation.

News Day competition

An annual News Day competition is an opportunity to create a newspaper or set of web pages reflecting current news, and is designed to be completed in a day. While previous preparation of templates, a collection of graphics and training on software and layout are also great learning opportunities, there is something to be said for the spontaneity and energy generated by an imminent and compulsory deadline. Sometimes creativity and imagination thrive under pressure.

If some of these activities seem a bit uncontrolled, I suppose that is one of the principles I am trying to emphasize. Discipline, regularity and consistency have their important place in learning, especially in our current formal education system, but some letting loose or breaking free, some frivolity and an occasional laid-back approach can reap immense dividends. While some pupils will probably take advantage, the overwhelming majority will learn something special. Switch off the bells, collapse the timetable for a day and let pupils take the opportunity to create. This is easier to achieve and more frequently done in a medium or small primary school, and I am sure that many secondary schools could learn from the approach.

Visits and visitors should be an integral part of the whole school curriculum, reflecting the school's relationship with the local community and beyond. They are an opportunity for the input of new ideas and experiences which can lead to creative thinking by teachers and pupils alike.

Creativity is closely linked to inclusion and differentiation as it gives a different opportunity for children to shine. The *Hard Times* extract in Chapter 1 shows Bitzer as a successful school pupil because he is well adapted to the rote learning of Mr Gradgrind's classroom. Sissy Jupe, on the other hand, knows the outside world, the countryside and horses and is a kinder and more imaginative person for that.

A creative environment is one where individuality is identified, nurtured and celebrated, where the needs of every child are met and where every child achieves according to their capabilities. It is one where there is a flexibility of approach as a response to many learning styles. And that creative environment is a successful learning environment.

Some classrooms don't encourage thinking. Repetitive exercises, too much routine and not enough challenge can make for an easy life, and one where thinking – and eventually learning – fade away. However, if children need to apply their thinking skills independently to issues, problems and to new situations, they will enhance their learning across a range of contexts.

The teacher's role is to provide opportunities for children to use their various thinking skills and to do so independently within a safe environment. Thinking may be more problem-solving or more philosophy (and there is a strong movement encouraging philosophy in the primary school) but either will help independent thought and lifelong learning.

It may seem unlikely to mention assessment here. Assessment

has become something of a bogey word and anathema to creativity. Where it is compared with the weighing of a pig (you don't fatten a pig by weighing it), I agree that constant assessment is bean counting for its own sake, yet assessment can be creative too. 'How long would it take five men to dig a hole three yards by four yards if . . .' is not the only way to assess someone's mathematical ability.

Where children actively participate in self-evaluative processes, helping to set their own targets and success criteria, reviewing their own work, using self and peer assessment, they are more involved in the process and are more likely to see it in a positive light.

If children are aware of their own learning styles and can reflect on their learning and identify their next steps, they are more likely to make progress.

Where teachers use formative assessment to plan future learning, we have the possibility of personal progress at an appropriate measured rate.

The pupil's voice can be heard in a creative classroom. It may be noisier and is probably less tidy than in a highly authoritarian classroom, but each child's contribution is valued. There is guided choice and some opportunity to choose outcomes, as they take part in developing a learning environment.

All this may take a bit more time than the headlong rush through the hoops and over the fences of National Curriculum statements, but the learning is deeper and longer lasting.

8

THE LEARNING-
CENTRED
ENVIRONMENT

Classrooms, playgrounds and playing fields, laboratories, studios and the home are all learning environments. In some places this environment is becoming impoverished in several ways. The urban environment is increasingly seen as a frightening place populated by asocial or anti-social groups. A Home Office report published in July 2005 shows that 47 per cent of all violent incidents were committed by a stranger, compared to 32 per cent in 1997. Woundings in the street rose from 20 per cent to 28 per cent between 1996 and 2003–4. Exactly 50 per cent of violent attacks by strangers were by an attacker who had been drinking. Little wonder, then, that caring parents try to keep their children away from the streets.

In *A Child's Place* (Thomas and Thompson 2004) by the Demos think tank, children were interviewed to determine their own views on their immediate environment. Asked how they would improve their environments, they said they wanted 'less traffic, better public transport, more green space, trees, dens, hiding places and less litter. Above all they wanted adults and other children to help protect their local environments.'

Schools where tarmac has been turned into real playgrounds by adding climbing frames, 'willow wombs' and by painting games on the hard surface are improving the learning environment. Where children themselves are involved in the consultations on what will be provided, there is the double opportunity of showing children that their ideas count and of gathering genuine evidence of what children want instead of what we think they ought to have.

Sadly, some school environments, especially some secondary schools, are not sympathetic to learning. After a while teachers and pupils can stop consciously noticing the depressing environment they are in, but it has an effect on their attitudes and their willingness to learn. I well remember a school where the Head's room was comfortable and well-presented while the staffroom had rickety coffee tables overflowing with cigarette ash, a sink full of dirty mugs and grey metal lockers lining the walls. The Head couldn't understand why I declined his offer of a job.

Similarly the classroom that welcomes the child with light and colour, and stimulates interest with displays and fresh air must generate more learning than a stale atmosphere with chewing gum on the carpets, stains on the walls and notices which are torn and tired.

I know this is a counsel of perfection because in many secondary schools teachers have to travel to several different classrooms and do not have the 'luxury' of their own room. However, it can be done and it is important it is done, even if this means appointing a member of a department to be responsible for displays and decoration. One of the reasons a visit to a primary school is generally positive is the pride the teachers take in their own rooms and the way this reflects their teaching and proudly presents the pupils' learning.

The climate of the classroom

The Hay, McBer Report (2000) emphasizes

> The quality of the learning environment is a key factor in determining pupil progress during a lesson. Good teachers create environments which maximise the pupils' opportunities to learn.

This kind of positive environment not only includes specifics such as air and light but also includes a sense of security and order, a stimulating place to be and an opportunity to participate actively in the class.

Hay, McBer identify nine 'climate dimensions'.

Climate dimension characteristics

Clarity – the purpose of the lesson is evident
Environment – the physical environment is attractive and stimulating
Fairness – the rewards given to the pupils match their actual performance
Interest – the classroom is an interesting place to be

Order – there is order in the classroom and control of the class
Participation – pupils are actively involved through questioning and discussion
Safety – pupils are not at risk from emotional or physical bullying
Standards – the standards to which each pupil should aspire to are made explicit
Support – pupils feel supported and are prepared to take risks

Displays

These should be appropriate to current learning, be learning resources in their own right, be opportunities for pupils to present their own work, be on general display to the whole school as well as in the classroom. While naturally you may be conscious of creating displays for parents' evenings or inspectors' visits, ideally the displays should come from the learning taking place with pupils and should be generated by and for them.

Books

Cicero famously said, 'a room without books is as a body without a soul' and many people would agree this is true of the learning environment. Too often, however, books in schools can be old, worn or irrelevant.

A resource-centred classroom might consider having tables for resources, shelves for books and trays for papers, with pupils expected to collect and interrogate resources as appropriate for their work.

My resources centre was ideal for this with an extensive variety of materials of different types on the shelves, clippings in filing cabinets and software and Internet access at computers, all in the same space.

We should all have access to this range of materials but too many of us inhabit sterile and uninspiring classrooms, owned by no one as we move from room to room. On the other hand a primary school classroom with a book box, wall displays and collections of exhibits and scrapbooks can supply most needs for a class while giving pupils the benefit of a guided choice and the atmosphere of a learning classroom.

While on the subject, how often do our pupils see us enjoying reading a book? Reading time is not a time to catch up on our admin or our marking, but a time for everyone to read – alone but knowing the rest of the class is reading too. Some schools have a simultaneous reading time for the whole school, when everyone, office staff, teachers and pupils, all pick up a book and read for half an hour. Idealistic? It can be, and has been, done!

Furniture and decoration

Damage and breakages should be reported promptly to site managers. Graffiti encourages more graffiti and must be stopped. Scrubbing desks and cleaning walls, and replacing damaged notices should not be necessary in a positive learning environment, but this is sadly a fact of life in many places. It reflects badly on teachers and pupils and starts a decline in standards which it is difficult to reverse.

There is a lot to be said for tables. They can seat two pupils, be moved into a variety of combinations in the room and out of it, but the standard metal framed tables with Formica tops are structurally unsound when leant against or sat upon by a hefty adolescent. Similarly, plastic and metal chairs are weakest when rocked backwards. The school desk *circa* 1950 that I bought from my first teaching post remains as strong as ever, with stout metal bars holding the seat to the capacious desk and lid. These old-fashioned desks have the virtue of keeping pupils singly in disciplined rows, though of course they don't have the flexibility needed for group work.

Decoration in some schools is based on an institutional theme of magnolia. However, pastel shades are well known to be more soothing and induce positive learning.

Carpets are a subject of much discussion. Hard surfaces are undoubtedly more practical, though noisier, and almost certainly best for public areas and thoroughfares, but carpeting is more congenial, quieter and welcoming in an office or classroom. However, a school which is unable to staunch the flow of chewing gum and ground-in food and drink can expect to have ugly and even hazardous flooring before long.

Once again the situation is down to a general positive school attitude, clear and policed rules, and the ability of individual teachers to enforce those rules in their own rooms. When this becomes personal, because we are house-proud and insist on high standards, learning will benefit.

Air and heating

There may not be much an individual teacher can do about this apart from reporting and following up damage, but clearing the air by opening doors and windows will clear the minds of the pupils and teacher too. Too hot or too cold and learning certainly suffers and, though this can often be used as an excuse by pupils looking for a reason not to work, the result is the same – a poor environment leads to poor learning.

Some educationalists have suggested that certain smells improve learning effectiveness. It might be possible to introduce an air freshener of rosemary and lemon to improve concentration or basil to clear the mind, but there is also the possibility of fielding complaints from asthmatic or allergic pupils. Certainly, fresh green plants and humidifiers can have a positive effect on the air balance and ozone in the air.

Simplest of all is to take a real break and trot with the whole class in tow around the school before returning to the classroom. Or abandon the classroom altogether for a while (see below).

Lighting and colour

Stygian gloom lit by broken fluorescent tubes would make an effective scene for a dystopian movie set, but is all too common in some schools. Modern lighting reflectors diffuse light more efficiently than those of 20 years ago, so they should be preferred where natural light is not sufficiently available. Experiments in schools in Devon and Exeter have produced a calm atmosphere and less disruption. Designer Mark Green used mostly yellow and red palettes for very young children who tend to prefer primary colours, and blue tones for older children who prefer more muted colours. This is on the basis that warm and vibrant colours encourage extrovert behaviour and cooler greens and blues promote calmness.

Noise, sound, music

Experiments have shown that the mustic of Mozart, played to children in the womb and also to children who found concentration and learning difficult, had a positive effect. Appropriate, relaxing music has a physiological effect which can turn into a positive learning atmosphere, especially when played as pupils enter the room or begin working. Remember that shops sometimes try the same device and note that some music will jar with you and at higher volumes will have an opposite effect.

Music at different volumes and of different types can either help concentration, relaxation, inspiration or motivation, so choose your music with care.

You might even try natural sounds such as birdsong and bubbling streams (though be prepared for some who need to visit the loo!). One of my regular lessons was to show slides of waves, water and the sea while playing Fleetwood Mac's relaxing 'Albatross' and natural wave sounds. Not only did I get good creative writing, but it was invariably a most relaxing and peaceful lesson!

It is not superfluous to mention that it is important that pupils have enforced, silent working time in which they can concentrate on their own work. Elsewhere I have said that negotiation and group work are important, but there is a balance which includes solo, concentrated work, enforced appropriately by a teacher who has set an appropriate task and will not accept any distractions. Pupils who routinely live in rooms with loud music, houses with televisions always on and areas where there is constant traffic noise, not to mention sports halls, discos and school canteens, are unused to silence or even quiet.

Enforce silence by:

- marking a clock on the board and adding a minute for each breach of silence, to be added on after the normal end of the lesson.
- adopting the custom of holding up your hand and having pupils raise their hands to be silent. Accept no delays. Adopt a fierce gaze.
- saying in a normal voice to the people nearest you that you want silence, you will have silence now and that otherwise the lesson will continue until breaktime. Do not raise your voice. Do expect that the message will be passed back by those in the front row. Use eye contact to reinforce your wishes.

Abandoning the classroom

Leaving the classroom entirely is a great stimulant of imagination and excitement. Don't be put off if at first the class seems uncontrolled – it could be because they have been cooped up within four walls for too long.

Short of a fully fledged field trip, if there is a park or garden nearby or if your school grounds have suitable areas, try taking the class out for a stroll. English teachers will find that a short preamble about using the five senses to describe the world around us can lead to a word-collecting activity as pupils listen, look, smell, taste and touch their environment. Stopping silently to listen and then record what they hear is sadly unnatural for many young people, and choosing words to describe what their senses tell them is an important exercise in building vocabulary and a strong link to what other authors have written.

Other activities which need no transport and can be done in a double lesson or together with another cooperative teacher over two lessons include:

- traffic-counting exercises
- questionnaires
- surveys of shopping provision
- surveys of housing types
- counting the number of plant species in a square metre
- guided tours of their local environment for items of historical interest
- pond dipping
- photographic essays on themes, e.g. the number 4, the letter A, doors, windows, circular patterns, motifs used in the built environment, triangles in nature ...

All of these get the children out of the classroom and into another, possibly richer, learning environment.

Flexible learning

A movement called Flexible Learning grew from research at the University of Sussex in the late 1980s. Many of the features of Flexible Learning occur elsewhere in this book, now absorbed in everyday education. Nevertheless it is worth recapping what was then – and is still now in some places – a radical focus on learning. Teachers of GNVQ courses may have absorbed already many of the principles here.

Flexible Learning's most obvious identifying features are:

The Management of Learning
The organized arrangement of differentiated activities, reviewing progress, keeping records. Activities will include work placements, community relationships, parental contacts, use of external facilities.

Organization of learning resources
Giving ready access to relevant and appropriate materials, including study packs and guided learning modules. This could be in the learning-focused classroom or in a specialized facility such as an art room, science lab or learning resources centre. The

same applies to open areas outside of classrooms. Classroom layout is now typically less formal than the traditional classroom and is likely to be open enough to incorporate visitors from the community coming in and pupils going out to access specialized resources or facilities.

The role of the teacher

Typically, the teacher is seen as a facilitator and adviser as much as an information giver (which is also necessary). Regular tutorials, one-to-one or in small groups, help develop a relationship with the learner and, during these, reviews and target-setting can take place at a personal level, agreed and negotiated where possible. A negotiated goal can be formalized into an agreed contract. Peer tutoring can also be used to support pupils for particular skills.

Increased pupil activity

As pupils become more responsible for their own learning and start finding out for themselves rather than being given answers, they begin to participate actively in their own learning rather than being passive recipients. This is a form of pupil autonomy, though learning is guided by the teacher and support can always be called upon. It also enables differentiation and a longer-term ability to manage one's own learning by self-assessment, which is the ultimate goal.

A combination of pupils being responsible for their own learning and a wide variety of activities and resources on offer mean that individual learning styles are catered for implicitly. The flexibility lies in a willingness to offer a variety of routes to the same goal.

Health and diet

Regular sleeping habits, exercise and a good breakfast are important factors in effective learning. While we only see our pupils for a fraction of each day, we experience the effects of their eating and sleeping habits. A deficiency of omega-3 fatty acids has an effect on attention spans and consequently on learning effectiveness.

Learning takes place most effectively in conditions where attention span can be maintained, and distractions and discomfort are minimized or coped with. So it makes sense if we can teach good habits of health and diet to our pupils and their parents.

The diet of English school children has been much discussed in recent years, but the knowledge that diet affects concentration and learning is not new. The sparse diet of World War Two caused some improvements in the nation's health, particularly with a reduction in sugar intake. After the war, free cod-liver oil and orange juice boosted levels of vitamin A and D, and studies have shown clear evidence of improvement in many children's concentration and behaviour when a 10 ml daily supplement of omega-3 is taken over six weeks.

Omega-3 is present in oily fish such as salmon, mackerel, sardines and tuna and is important for brain-cell development. A school and home that encourage healthy eating will make a significant difference to pupils' learning.

- Give publicity in the school canteen to healthy foods
- Use the same publicity to inform parents
- Reduce or eliminate fatty and sugary foods from the canteen menu
- Provide interesting, tasty and fresh foods
- Publicize the changes in school assemblies
- Explain the changes in food lessons, making the emphasis on nutrition and health at least as much as on process and technology
- Hold after-school cookery clubs
- Make eating an enjoyable and social occasion, both at home and at school

And for health:

- Build more activity into the school day
- Provide safe and interesting activity areas in the school grounds

147

- Encourage participation in sports and games irrespective of whether you represent the school
- Encourage parents to use the walking bus scheme and have their children walk to school

Parents can be encouraged to:

- make home-made soups and stews using vegetables
- offer raw vegetables as snacky food with dips
- offer snacks such as dried fruit and fresh fruit

and to offer simple unprocessed meals such as:

- tinned salmon mixed with sweetcorn and a little mayonnaise
- top a ready-made pizza base with tomato purée, peppers, sweetcorn, onions, tinned tuna and low-fat cheese, then grill it
- a baked potato, the flesh removed and mixed with tinned tuna, chopped spring onions and grated cheese, and then put back into the potato skin and grilled.

Diet and memory

Many studies have shown that eating breakfast improves memory. However, many children come to school without having eaten – or having snacked on sweets or crisps. Our brain comprises 2 per cent of our body's weight, but it uses 20–30 per cent of our body's energy. Clearly feeding it with the right food should be a priority. Glucose has been found to enhance learning and memory, but straight sugar only gives a boost for a very short time.

For example, Carol Greenwood, Professor of Nutrition at the University of Toronto, gave a group of healthy people a bowl of cereal and milk, along with white grape juice for breakfast. Another group only drank water. When tested 20 minutes later, the cereal eaters were able to remember 25 per cent more facts.

Diet and behaviour

Children's behaviour often deteriorates in the late morning and late afternoon, or three to four hours after a meal, when blood-sugar levels fall. Mid-morning snacks can reduce the problem; so, when considering the litter problem around school at break time, balance that with the knowledge that children's classroom behaviour and learning potential may be improving.

It's possible for parents and older pupils to plan their meals according to how they use their brain during the day. A low-calorie, high-protein meal which contains complex carbohydrates makes us more alert so would be ideal for breakfast and lunch. Dessert at lunchtime is likely to make us less alert in the afternoon. A higher-calorie, higher-carbohydrate, lower-protein meal helps us relax and may help us sleep in the evening. If you are fortunate enough to attend an in-service training course with hotel lunch you might bear this in mind when selecting from the menu!

Water, additives, colouring affecting behaviour

It's well known that food additives can affect behaviour. Many examples of hyperactivity are caused by too much sugar or colouring in a child's diet. Increasingly, water is recognized as an important part of the diet too.

Pupils need water for their health and to combat dehydration, which in turn affects their concentration. Provide drinking fountains, as they do in Australia and as was common in schools and in parks in the UK at one time. Allow water bottles in the classroom. Be alert in the early stages of introduction for incidents of splashing and squirting and warn pupils that this privilege will be withdrawn if the water is wrongly used. Encourage water rather than fizzy or coloured drinks, which contain sugars and additives which overstimulate, as well as being bad for young teeth.

Coffee, water and teacher voice care

Drinking more water has a number of benefits. For teachers this includes voice care. A teacher is a professional voice user, but continued overuse in large halls and dusty classrooms without time for recovery can result in serious damage to the throat and vocal cords. While there seems to be a reluctance to offer or accept serious voice training, as experienced by actors and singers, the very least a teacher should do is:

- drink water frequently, including during lessons
- avoid coffee during the day – it clogs up the throat; black tea is better, especially lapsang souchong, but water is best
- if you are addicted to coffee, add a sprinkling of cinnamon, which may increase your body's ability to use glucose and gives you a lift without sugar
- remember that caffeine dependence is quite common, while not in the same league as tobacco or alcohol, and that withdrawal, for example on holidays away from your staff-room routine, can bring about headaches, fatigue and depression.

You can also help voice care by:

- adopting a balanced posture when addressing a class and projecting your voice at or above their heads
- avoiding shouting as far as possible. This may seem unavoidable at times, but whistles are effective and other methods such as gestures and a penetrating stare have an important place
- preferring a deep voice to a high one – shrieking is damaging both for your voice and your relationships with children

How brains work

It has been said that by the age of 5 we have learned half of what we will ever learn. If we consider the importance of walking, talking, basic socialization, responding consciously to experience, etc., its significance must be far greater than learning the periodic table or the causes of the French Revolution. Even if we argue over the precise age and quantity of learning, it is irrefutable that children learn basic skills more rapidly than adults. The newborn child's brain weighs about a pound, but by six years old it weighs three pounds – at least partly accounted for by the process of learning.

Young children acquire language much more readily than do adults, and it is generally agreed that there are early critical or sensitive periods for language acquisition from about 12 months to six years. Children who are exposed to a language in the first six years quickly learn to speak that language effectively, while older children and adults may have difficulty with pronunciation and grammar which will mark them out as non-native speakers.

Critical periods in language acquisition vary according to circumstances but there is a gradual decline in language acquisition abilities over time. If a child has not learned language at all it is unlikely that it can be learned effectively after early adolescence, as exemplified by Victor, 'the Wild Boy of Aveyron', described by Rousseau; in *Savage Girls and Wild Boys* (2003) by Michael Newton; and by Genie, described by Russ Rymer in *Genie: A Scientific Tragedy* (1994), who were deprived of language in their formative years.

To some extent this is also true of other skills such as riding a bicycle and catching a ball, which become increasingly difficult or slower to master as age increases beyond puberty.

The lesson for teachers is that the earlier we can influence children the more effective can be their learning, although it is never too late. Two facts should give teachers cause for encouragement. First, it has been estimated that over 80 per cent of what we know about how the brain works has been discovered since the mid-1990s, and secondly, neuro-scientists estimate that that the average person uses only about 3 per cent of their brain capacity. Some scope for improvement, then.

Hay, McBer (2000) confirm:

teachers really do make a difference. Within their classrooms, effective teachers create learning environments which foster pupil progress by deploying their teaching skills as well as a wide range of professional characteristics. Outstanding teachers create an excellent classroom climate and achieve superior pupil progress largely by displaying more professional characteristics at higher levels of sophistication within a very structured learning environment. (para 1.1.9)

Research by Blakemore and Fritch (2000) suggests that the brain continues to be flexible throughout life and can change measurably as new skills are learnt.

Recent advances in brain mapping can identify specific areas of the brain, and may in time lead to highly targeted exercises to remedy specific learning difficulties.

The Institute of Child Health in London found that, at puberty, the ability to recognize the expressions on people's faces significantly declines, with boys finding it particularly difficult. Sadness and anger often go unnoticed because the brain is being 'rewired' due to genetic and hormonal changes. This could go some way to explain why the reactions of teachers and parents seem to be ignored by adolescents and may lead us to be more specific in our indications of disapproval at unacceptable behaviour.

We already know that there are differences between the left and right side of the brain:

The left brain is analytical, logical, precise and time-sensitive. The right brain is dreamier, it processes things in a holistic way ... is more emotional ...'

(Carter, *Mapping the Mind* , 1999)

Our learning styles may be governed by our preferences for left or right brain working. Experiments show that the two different sides, or hemispheres, of the brain are responsible for different ways of thinking – as shown in the table overleaf:

Left brain	Right brain
Logical	Random
Sequential	Intuitive
Rational	Holistic
Analytical	Synthesizing
Objective	Subjective
Looks at parts	Looks at wholes

Left-brain subjects such as maths and science focus on logical thinking, analysis and accuracy. Right-brain subjects, such as English and performing arts, focus on aesthetics, feeling and creativity. In general, schools tend to encourage left-brain modes of thinking, rather than right-brain modes. To encourage a more balanced 'whole-brain' approach we should be giving an equal emphasis to the creative and performing arts and treating them as equal in importance in our children's learning.

This might include introducing activities with more metaphors, analogies, role-playing, visual elements and movement into their reading, calculation and analytical activities, and building these skills into assessment.

Presentation

Dale's 'Cone of experience' (1969: 107) suggests that people remember:

- 10 per cent of what they read
- 20 per cent of what they hear
- 30 per cent of what they see
- 50 per cent of what they hear and see
- 70 per cent of what they say and write
- 90 per cent of what they say and perform at a task

In fact, an analysis by Work-Learning Research (2005) demonstrates that although the principle is correct, the percentages are false. Nevertheless, the general point is: 'Tell me and I'll forget. Show me and I'll remember. Involve me and I'll understand.'

The lesson for the classroom is obvious. While it's easy for us to talk, and quite easy to generate reading material and worksheets, the most effective learning activities involve the children doing things themselves, and perhaps teaching others what they themselves have found. It is more than likely that we all know this already, but in the relentless pace of the school we can forget the simple things in chasing the paper and ticking the boxes. Too often we wear ourselves out when we should have the pupils, not ourselves, working harder.

In the face of targets and inspectors we try to perform, when what we should be doing is making the pupils work (i.e. learn) more effectively.

Consistency

Perhaps the most important single attitude a teacher can bring to the classroom is consistency. Not repetitiveness, not dull repetition but a consistency of attitude. Where there is a lack of control at home or where adolescent hormones are fighting for space, it is consistency in standards, discipline and attitude which make the teacher a rock amidst a seething sea.

To be calm and constant in the face of bad behaviour or poor standards of work is not an easy task. It saps the spirits and weakens resolve, but when a pupil knows where he stands, knows that poor work will be returned for improvements, poor behaviour will be criticized or punished, in a consistent way, then that forms the basis of an agreement and an understanding which is the basis for respect and of learning. Do remember to criticize the behaviour, not the child. Most pupils have a sense of fairness and respect a fair teacher. It just doesn't always seem like that at the time.

Raising self-esteem

No one will do their best if they feel undervalued. Teachers know this all too well, and the same is true of our pupils.

It is true to say that deprivation comes not only from economic poverty but poverty of aspirations. Aspirations can be raised by valuing each child and their learning. Teachers can undermine children and the reverse is also true, but when they work together in a positive and purposeful atmosphere they can spark off great learning in each other – including a sense of self-worth.

- Generate a positive learning culture in the classroom and the school
- Ensure the work is relevant to the pupil, and explain how it is relevant if that's not obvious
- Set challenging but achievable targets for each pupil
- Value all contributions
- Provide positive feedback
- Avoid sarcasm
- Use praise as much as possible and always more than criticism
- Be aware of pupils' feelings
- Treat children as individuals
- Listen!

A strong sense of self-worth can come from the act of participating with others in purposeful tasks. A good classroom may have individual learning, but the collective experience of doing something together holds enormous benefits.

Using your library/resources centre

One of the strongest features of the learning-centred school should be the resources centre.

Many schools have made the change from library to resources centre, but even in schools where they have a great library/ resources centre it's not always used effectively. Sometimes this is because we aren't aware of what's available, sometimes because there is so much available that it is daunting and it seems easier to stay in the classroom.

The first person to speak to is your librarian. If you are a librarian you may have difficulty tracking down teachers to whom you can talk. After all, at lunch and break times, just when teachers pop out of the classroom and might be available in the staffroom, the librarian is busiest, dealing with the influx of pupils.

Whether you arrange an appointment or lie in wait for each other it is hugely important that teachers and librarians talk to each other, both formally and informally. Share wine and cheese in the library after school, meet up after the school day, attend meetings where your input is valued, talk about your holiday reading, whatever it takes to start a partnership.

This should lead on to shared preparation of projects, agreeing on what resources can be bought or borrowed well before a project starts and together enforcing a work ethic in the resources centre and delivery of information and study skills. The 'dream team' of librarian and teacher as fellow professionals offers a rich learning experience. From that come all sorts of benefits for staff and pupils alike.

Booking a timetable slot in the resources centre guarantees access to a wide range of resources in different media. A well-appointed room will offer a balance of multimedia, online, book and non-book resources. Following one of the models of information literacy, pupils will develop their information handling skills on a project or topic which is integral to their curriculum and which can here be learned through their own research. They are in fact learning how to learn.

Following the agreed school model for research will give structure to the activity and preparation might include:

- providing a variety of activities for pupils so that they don't all want the same resources at the same time.
- emphasizing and demonstrating that book-based research can be superior to research using the Internet.
- ensuring pupils don't hog the computers; while every child

should have the opportunity to do sensible focused research on the Internet, every child should also use non-computer resources too.

- ensuring pupils know how to ask questions to target their searches.
- being very clear about what makes a good question. 'I want to know everything about the Victorians' is a bad task; 'I want to find out about living conditions for a ten-year-old child in 1850s London, written in the form of the child's personal diary' is a good task.
- providing a starter list of recommended websites for this topic – uploaded to the school intranet or website where possible.

Barriers to learning

Barriers to learning can be overcome, or at least faced up to. Once you know what the problem is you're half way there with solving it. After all, Helen Keller was taught to read and write.

While you as a teacher may be unable or unwilling to get involved in solving out-of-school problems such as poor nutrition, unsuitable housing, lack of medical and parental care, abuse or racial and cultural discrimination, any of these will be bound to have an impact on your pupils' ability to learn.

We are in a position to mediate with parents or to inform relevant services if we think there is a cause for concern. We may be an appropriate confidante or simply an observer, but it is important that we don't ignore our role. We may not be as involved as Mr Farthing in Barry Hines' *Kes*, but can play a vital role. Most schools have named persons for specialist counselling and it is important that, when issues of bereavement, suspected drug abuse or child abuse arise, these fellow professionals should be alerted straight away. As holders of sensitive information they may already know about the case and be able to advise you immediately on the next step.

I remember being very troubled by a story written by a Year 10 pupil describing abuse she received at home. My school's counsellor was able to assure me that the child was a fantasist, as she already knew the background. Family liaison may be better left to the specialist, though not everyone will agree.

Inclusion

This thorny issue polarizes those who believe the best thing for all pupils is to be together and those who don't. Wheelchair access, sound loops for the hard of hearing and bright stripes for the partially sighted can ease the way for children with restricted physical abilities, making it easier for them to join their peers and share the learning experiences. Pupils with learning disabilities pose a different problem. Where integration in the school community is a plus for the majority, it can pose problems for classroom organization. It is certainly easier to teach pupils who are of similar abilities, and more difficult – though by no means impossible – to arrange differentiated learning.

Resources

UK schools are generally well funded. There, I've said it! But I was very restricted by a lack of funding for many years in my large secondary school. There are considerable inequalities in funding provision between different parts of the country and this seems politically an intractable issue. Certainly a Head with sufficient clout and drive can extract money in exchange for participation in projects or making partnerships with the right people. Sometimes these projects themselves also enhance learning, though some would see that sponsorship brings with it the risk of selling your soul!

Behaviour and attendance

Either home and family issues or school issues can lead to low attendance or unacceptable behaviour. While behaviour management strategies can help in the classroom, often the real problem lies elsewhere. That doesn't mean unacceptable behaviour in the classroom can be tolerated, but it does mean we may have to accept that we can't solve a problem whose roots lie elsewhere.

Medical disorders affecting learning

These should be picked up by the school system or reported, as a matter of routine and a matter of importance. Dyslexia, dyspraxia, attention deficit, hyperactivity disorder (AD, HD) Asperger's syndrome, etc., cannot be solved by teachers but can be coped with in the classroom with suitable help from teaching assistants, local authority services and information from dedicated support groups and their extensive websites. Specific physical medical problems can be met with adapted learning conditions – a hearing aid, large text screens, individual work or a quiet room for a sufferer from dismenorrhea or migraine. The difficulty arises where you or a parent suspect a medical problem, but you can't receive a definitive diagnosis. This led to dyslexia being described as a 'middle-class disease' when concerned parents used it to excuse children's poor spelling, and to chronic fatigue syndrome being labelled 'yuppie flu'.

Illegal drug use

Unquestionably this will have an effect on learning as it will influence a child personally and socially, mentally and physically. The effects can vary from overexcitability to being withdrawn, but certainly mood changes, already a feature of adolescence, can become even greater in a pupil using illegal drugs.

Schools have a vital role in educating children about the consequences of drug-taking, in identifying behaviour which suggests illegal drug use, and in either coping with it or excluding the pupil. If drug use becomes a focus for a child, classroom learning is likely to suffer.

Bullying

This is mentioned elsewhere and is certainly a cause of some children hating school, not succeeding, not attending. Anti-bullying peer groups supported by suitably experienced adult staff are a very effective solution. A whole-school policy against bullying must be translated into practicality and children must know that bullying will not be tolerated and what to do if it takes place.

Family and home

It is important that the school intervenes, even if it cannot solve a problem. Keeping in touch with home can be a lifeline, a vital connection for a distressed family, though it need not – probably should not – be the role of the school to solve family problems. Alerting social services and acting as a conduit for information if necessary is an excellent role. Teachers are often blamed for the troubles of society; that's because we are in the middle of them all. But it should not be a sign to us that we can actually solve all of society's problems ourselves.

Motivation

This connects to many of the features above. A love of learning may be driven by any number of influences, from parents and family members through chance encounters at an impression-able time with inspiring teachers. Teachers can motivate pupils by personal qualities such as honesty, integrity, sympathy, patience; or professional skills such as the ability to convey complex topics with clarity, the power to hold pupils' attention, grasp of the subject matter. Sometimes motivation is an enthusiasm to achieve short-term targets. Inspiring pupils for a year at a time is far beyond what so-called motivational speakers and preachers achieve, but sometimes it can last for a lifetime.

Emerging technologies and distributed learning

Computers have brought us writing and editing tools, the Internet, communication tools and new educational environments. Virtual reality is already here in some forms and new types of messages and experiences are now common in our classrooms.

These new experiences have the potential for lively, innovative and significant learning, if properly handled. However, the pedagogy for the new media is still being researched and has often not trickled down to the classroom teacher.

The potential of the new media lies in ways of extending traditional learning into communication with larger, more distant and more varied groups and audiences. This communication can be synchronous (in real time, such as Chat or video conferencing) or asynchronous (such as threaded email discussions). Discussions can be one to one, one to many, or many to many. Distance education, once limited by paper and the postal service can become a lively medium in which dispersed learners exist as an online group or virtual community to share, discuss and interact across distance and time. This is learning, which, when complemented by multimedia simulations, offers the potential of learning environments anywhere at any time, with core resources being added to or even taken over by the empowered participants. Dede (1996) on distributed learning and Tiffin and Rajasingham (1995) describing virtual-reality classrooms, paint colourful pictures of stimulating and innovative educational environments within which learning could thrive.

Virtual Learning Environments

We can also add Virtual Learning Environments (VLEs) or Learning Platforms. These also appear as Managed Learning Environments to reflect the fact that they need considerable input from teachers to make appropriate materials available and to develop ways of working within them.

VLEs offer technology-mediated support for the learning process by linking teacher, learner and resources together with a variety of communications systems, assessment features and administration systems. They store and deliver information, they offer guidance and help and they facilitate communication and discussion.

Virtual Learning Environments may offer:

- A bank of core learning materials, such as lecture notes, PowerPoint presentations and video clips. More elaborately this might be access to mapped elements of the curriculum, which can be individually assessed and recorded. Routes through the learning units will be provided.
- Links to additional quality assured resources which support online courses given by the school or college.
- Communications, which may be synchronous/asynchronous, tutor–pupil, pupil–tutor, pupil–pupil, one to one or many to many. These can be text-based (chat, threaded discussion or conventional email) or can be video-based. They can be limited to a small group or extended far afield. They can be live or archived for future retrieval.
- Tools for creating your own interactive and multimedia course materials which can be adapted to the needs of individual learners.
- Online assessment – both formative and summative.
- Collaborative tools such as the ability to discuss online, share materials and edit each other's work. One popular tool is the shared whiteboard on which one member can write while others see the result, in real time.
- Links to administration and management systems so an administrator can keep track of progress and offer support.

Currently these are being used in further and higher education and are moving into sixth-form colleges where large numbers of dispersed learners need similar facilities to universities. There is some potential, for example, for use in sixth forms where it can be uneconomical to run a course with few candidates but where a single teacher can teach a number of dispersed candidates through online distance learning.

There has been some success with younger pupils judged to be 'gifted and talented' and whose abilities in mathematics have been stretched by joining an online maths group with a single teacher.

VLEs are not a panacea, however. A major weakness of online learning seems to be motivation, which is hard to maintain without face-to-face encounters. Most successful distance learning incorporates some actual meetings to complement the virtual encounters, following the example of the highly successful Open University summer schools. The teacher or tutor plays a vital part in keeping in touch with the student personally, by phone and by email, checking on progress and charting progress electronically.

Computer games and learning

A large proportion of young people, more boys than girls, play computer games. Clearly they are entertained, but do these games actually help or hinder the ability of children to learn?

Kirriemuir and McFarlane (2004) say 'The experience of game play seems to be affecting learners' expectations of learning activities. Preferred tasks are fast, active and exploratory, with information supplied in multiple forms in parallel.'

They point out that children can become involved in these games to the point where they are oblivious to distractions. The fantasy, challenge and curiosity involved in gaming encourages concentration to sometimes obsessive levels. The games require an active response, unlike many television programmes, for example. They encourage useful skills such as:

- strategic thinking
- planning
- communication
- application of numbers
- negotiating skills
- group decision-making
- data-handling

Television's professional presentation techniques and dramatic re-enactments have been seen as a challenge for the class teacher who cannot hope to compete on a daily basis with the resources and skills of the likes of the BBC. Is it possible that we are again outplayed by games manufacturers – or is this an area where we can adapt our learning techniques?

Computer games clearly motivate children, which is something we would want to encourage. Simulations certainly involve children asking questions and experiencing environments and events outside their usual experience. Can we also learn from the way they use levels and scores to encourage children to achieve more?

Kirriemuir and McFarlane (2004) quote Malone (1980):

- the activity should be structured so that the player can increase or decrease the level of challenges faced, in order to match exactly personal skills with the requirements for action
- it should be easy to isolate the activity, at least at the perceptual level, from other stimuli, external or internal, which might interfere with involvement in it
- there should be clear criteria for performance; a player should be able to evaluate how well or how poorly (s)he is doing at any time
- the activity should provide concrete feedback to the player, so that (s)he can tell how well (s)he is meeting the criteria of performance
- the activity ought to have a broad range of challenges, and possibly several qualitatively different ranges of challenge, so that the player may obtain increasingly complex information about different aspects of her/himself

Teachers have always pounced on current trends to introduce relevance to the classroom and to help effective learning. Computer games are another advanced technology intended to entertain but capable of stimulating learning. Not all the genres of gaming are suitable for classroom use and some are notably violent in theme, but the Myst, Riven and Uru series of quests and the SIM simulations have clear and immediate benefits, especially when they become collaborative rather than solitary activities.

With the use of a wireless or infrared keyboard and mouse, an adventure game can be played by a whole class, with teacher mediating to help the group come to joint decisions. Joint decision-making in an adventure or simulation is a very cooperative experience.

The electronic portfolio

Once upon a time pupils had exercise books for skills exercises and neat writing, while jotters were reserved for rough work. Later, work was done on paper which could be punched and inserted in loose-leaf files. Similar paper was used for handouts, notes and essays so the material could be arranged in any appropriate order. Course work could also be completed on file paper but was sometimes submitted on different sizes and colours of paper as display quality competed with content for the attention of the moderator. An electronic portfolio has several advantages over these previous media while incorporating their best qualities. Government has suggested that every child should have an online area of their own by 2008 and there is already software for simplifying the creation and storage of online media for children.

An electronic portfolio can:

- be copied and backed up so it is less likely to be lost
- be viewed on screen or on a printed page as appropriate
- feature colour and multimedia if required
- use one piece of work in several places if required – so the piece of writing on First World War Poetry can be used for assessment in both English and history. Similarly a piece of work produced cooperatively by more than one pupil could be either copied to all the owners' folders or linked to from a central point
- incorporate storage of previous work, whether completed or in draft stage

- store electronic files methodically using a uniform pattern across all subject departments. This makes it easier for new teachers to see what has been done previously
- be displayed in chronological order to show development and improvement. This is particularly important for new teachers previewing their pupils' previous work
- be reorganized in any new way according to the needs of assessment, new syllabus requirements, etc.
- be always available for viewing by teachers, the pupil, moderators and examiners

To ensure conformity across the school it is easy to set up a basic pattern when pupils first access their account. For a Year 7 pupil this could consist of one main folder for all their work and subfolders for each of their timetable subjects. A sample of their best primary school work could be forwarded to the secondary school to await their arrival. Further subfolders could easily be added for careers, pastoral topics, copies of reports, etc. Much of this could form the basis of a regularly updated Record of Achievement. Naturally nothing in the folders should contravene the *Data Protection Act* or copyright (no problem if it is all the pupil's own work) or in any way jeopardize the administration network if this is separate from the curriculum network, and where formal copies of reports, absences and official school records are held.

There are several ways to set up a standard portfolio. Taking the basic pattern outlined above and applying this to all new accounts will create a framework.

Within that it is useful to provide a contents page leading to general sub areas and to specific files. This would be edited by the pupil as the collection grows.

A word-processor contents page

This would have the advantage of a simple front page on which pupils write the titles of the work they want to include, to which they would create links by hypertext. This would seem to be the safe choice.

A web-page contents page

This would do the same thing but with more complexity – yet more flexibility. It would need simple web-editing software and would be more adaptable by those interested in extending their abilities by adding graphics, animations and multimedia.

In either option, links could be made to electronic files of all kinds including web pages created by the pupils themselves, videos of performances stored in a central place for use by all participants, etc.

Technology skills

Five technological capabilities

In order of advancement:

- Awareness   recognize the new technologies and their applications
- User   use technology to support learning
- Maker   apply the technology to a variety of appropriate situations
- Evaluator   make critical judgements about technology in use
- Holistic   recognize the impact of technology on how we think and learn

Teachers should aim to achieve these capabilities if they are to pass on their awareness to pupils.

These five technological capabilities highlight the fact that just using a computer – even having mastered word-processing software – does not make us very capable.

We can encourage higher-level skills in our pupils by

- giving them details of their task
- having them choose the most suitable software for their task

- having them justify their choice
- watching them follow their choice
- having them evaluate their choice after the task is complete

Telling them to open a particular piece of software and proceed in this or that way is less encouraging of higher ICT skills than setting a task and inviting them to create a variety of solutions.

In this way pupils can follow their interests and create an interactive story in a web editor or presentation software instead of a word processor. They might create lists in a spreadsheet with more inventive features than a flat table surrounded by text.

Encouraged to evaluate their own and each others work, they can gain greater insight than if they are shoehorned into a conventional write > submit > get marked process.

One good exercise is to play 'how many ways of ... using computer software?'

How many ways can you think of:

- telling a story
- connecting up ideas
- explaining a process
- warning people
- advertising an event

Include both computer-based and other means, then concentrate on how – or if – the computer might do the job more effectively and finally which method and what software would be most useful. Remember that it is as important to know when *not* to use a computer as it is to know when to use it appropriately.

ICT is not simply a conduit for delivering content, but a powerful tool for enhancing our thinking and our learning. Where the Plowden Report called for learning by doing, this post-Plowden ICT revolution can call for making and producing because computers now make the necessary tools available.

Ofsted states that ICT supports the following areas best of all:

- Information literacy
- Collaborative working

- Thinking skills
- Independent learning
- Media literacy
- Visualization
- Creativity

How can we introduce the technological capabilities to our pupils?

- Invite suggestions for the best software to fulfil a task
- Provide the opportunity of evaluating their own and their peers' work
- Avoid limiting tasks to traditional media
- Encourage use of multimedia presentations
- Have an electronic portfolio for each child
- Encourage pupils to reflect on what they have learned and how they might use their newly learned skills elsewhere

Use

- sound and music, whether electronic, sampled or real
- video of activity, process, dance and movement, storytelling, acting, animation
- graphics, drawings that are scanned, drawn or filtered, in all subjects whenever this enhances the message

Thinking skills

Thinking skills have been referred to elsewhere, but here is a list of major thinking skills that learners would need as designers of multimedia presentations (Carver *et al.* 1992):

Project-management skills

- creating a timeline for the completion of the project
- allocating resources and time to different parts of the project
- assigning roles to team members

Research skills

- determining the nature of the problem and how research should be organized
- posing thoughtful questions about structure, models, cases, values and roles
- searching for information using text, electronic and pictorial information sources
- developing new information with interviews, questionnaires and other survey methods
- analysing and interpreting all the information collected to identify and interpret patterns

Organization and representation skills

- deciding how to segment and sequence information to make it understandable
- deciding how information will be represented (text, pictures, movies, audio, etc.)
- deciding how the information will be organized (hierarchy, sequence) and how it will be linked

Presentation skills

- mapping the design onto the presentation and implementing the ideas in multimedia
- attracting and maintaining the interests of the intended audiences

Reflection skills

- evaluating the program and the process used to create it
- revising the design of the program using feedback

Many of these skills have already been mentioned in previous chapters, but here they show how a collaborative project such as designing a multimedia presentation on a given topic would offer considerable learning opportunities and a means of practising significant skills.

Rupert Wegerif, in quoting the above list of skills asks 'Could not all of these skills equally be developed through designing and making a poster display?' Of course, he is probably right, and the activities using skills are the most important thing. However, the ICT element serves to give opportunities for different skills and means the end product could have more impact and the contents could be repurposed for a variety of end products (presentation, web pages, online booklet, etc.) and different audiences.

Basic versus advanced skills

While some schools are lucky to have ample ICT facilities, even to the extent of wireless connected laptops for every child, most schools have to ration their limited facilities.

One effective secondary school model which teaches basic computer skills then incorporates them into general learning is as follows:

- Dedicated lessons by skilled teachers throughout Year 7 covering:
  - Word processing
  - Graphics
  - Desktop publishing
  - Internet use
  - Information handling
  - Spreadsheets
  - Databases
- Subsequent ICT use would be largely integrated into existing subjects, where ICT would, ideally, be used to develop, reinforce and enhance the curriculum of the subject area.
- This would be supported by drop-in facilities when occasional individual use is needed.

Computer software and the skills of using it can help make learning more effective. In some cases they can make learning possible for the first time. The help and flexibility that a word processor gives to a writer (especially this one) is incalculable, given that it can combine separate documents, enable invisible editing, high-quality output and layout. Of course, the writer still needs inspiration and ability, but the word processor is an enormous help to a writer of any standard, as is a spreadsheet to those who struggle with mathematical calculations. Any kind of sorting, searching, reordering and combining of data is made easier by word processors, spreadsheets and databases.

Repurposing such as converting a plain text file into an attractive brochure or an interactive presentation is made easier because there is no need to retype.

Word processing

Enables the manipulation, editing and formatting of text. This in turn encourages experimentation, potentially leading to creativity. Particular features include:

Drag and drop, cut and paste
Moving text around easily avoids the traditional barrier to handwritten text, the tedium of rewriting.

Outline view
Which allows students to plan their writing in a framework.

Tracking changes
Which keeps track of amendments whether by a single writer or a group writing cooperatively.

Highlighting
Helps to mark text for discussion or revision.

Search and replace
Searching for words and phrases in a long document, and the replacing one word with another, add functionality to the

writing process. The search facility can search for highlighted text as well as particular words and specific formats.

Formatting
Text can be redesigned in appearance without wholesale rewriting. Layout contributes to language style and meaning.

Graphics

While graphics software does not make users into artists or designers, any more than a word processor makes a user into an author, using and adapting existing graphics is easy enough to encourage writers to add design elements to their work, to illustrate words with pictures, and therefore potentially to enhance communication.

Desktop publishing

This was once a distinct and different kind of software. However, programs like Word now have such advanced tools that combining text and graphics has moved into the field of word processing. Experimenting with the effects of text and graphics together can lead to a much greater appreciation of design as communication.

Spreadsheets

Magical generators of calculations (just showing a simple spreadsheet to a pupil whose maths skills are weak can stimulate real interest), a spreadsheet can also demonstrate 'what if' ideas. For example, if I get 10 per cent more pocket money and buy fewer sweets will I have enough left over to go to the cinema once a month? A spreadsheet can keep track of changing figures without rewriting the whole table.

Charts and graphs
Can also be created using spreadsheet data.

Presentation

PowerPoint is the best known but not the only presentation software. Commonly used for business presentations, pupils can easily generate their own presentations to enhance talks or demonstrate ideas as a real alternative to more traditional essays. Illustrating the background to civil rights in the United States is greatly enhanced by photographs, maps and documents of the time, available on the Internet and repurposed by a pupil.

Databases

Collect and arrange information in a variety of ways. A database of a pupil's music collection can be arranged in a spreadsheet or a database while a database may be better suited to including graphics – a football player's match record including photographs, for example. Collaborative projects such as compiling class book reviews make good use of databases. A simplified graphical database such as Viewpoint is likely to appeal to the non-expert rather than the more powerful but impenetrable Microsoft Access.

Projectors and whiteboards

Teachers and pupils alike can display their work using projectors, but interactive whiteboards encourage collaborative input and sharing multimedia resources. Interactive whiteboards and wireless linked tablets have released the computer from the single and personal screen to become a whole class collaboration area.

Cameras and scanners

Provide the original graphics (and OCR text) which personalize a daily diary, a story or a database. The pictures can be edited in a graphics program or even in a word processor using drawing tools.

Using photo effects in Word

Search engines such as *Google Image Search* can also find images on almost any topic which can then be repurposed and edited (subject to copyright).

WebQuests

A WebQuest is a kind of guided Internet treasure hunt. Guided because it can offer a framework like those I've suggested in Chapter 4 and give links to suitable sites and resources to guide pupils and avoid aimless 'surfing'. Most WebQuests have the following six steps:

Introduction
The stimulus material that acts as a 'hook' for the pupil and involves them with the task. This could be a real-life situation or a fantasy scenario.

Task
This should have a realistic and achievable outcome, but could take a variety of formats. See Chapter 10 for a wide range of end-

products which go beyond the traditional 'write a story' or the meaningless 'find out everything you can about ...'

Process

The WebQuest guides the pupil through a step-by-step process to help them to complete the task. Pupils can work individually or as part of a larger group with individually assigned roles.

The process should be clear and should provide guidance on how to complete the task, for example by providing guide sheets or mini tasks on skills such as those in Chapters 4 and 5.

Resources

A WebQuest uses the Internet as its main, though not only, resource bank. Hyperlinks from a main page on the school's own website or one of the sites described in the WebQuests list at the end of this book (p. 216), guide pupils to the most appropriate resources, which can be differentiated and appropriate to ability.

Evaluation

Here pupils see the criteria on which their work will be assessed, whether their individual work or their contribution to a team. Pupils can reflect on this and review what they are doing by looking at what is judged to be successful.

Conclusion

Finally the pupil can evaluate progress and either revise what they have done or explore further.

Examinations and tests

These encourage students to work towards a clear goal at a specific time. They also help to verify that students can produce appropriate answers on their own and at a standard which can be standardized and compared with other students. On the other hand they do cause stress and are often seen as artificial, especially by students about to sit them.

A balanced view would appreciate that some stress is not a bad thing and that timed examinations taken with a broader assessment of continuous coursework give a pretty good overall picture of a student's ability. Once we have accepted that there is a place for a timed examination, what then can we do to make the most of the examination?

Teacher

- accept the inevitability of examinations and assert their value in assessing skills
- provide regular short tests which require some revision and can be easily marked
- point out that work learned early reduces stress when the exam arrives
- provide timed essay practice nearer the time of examinations
- when teaching, make clear where the topic stands as part of the overall syllabus
- as examination time approaches, increase positive encouragement

Pupil

- start learning early – don't wait until the last moment
- create a timetable of learning and revision for the weeks and months before the examinations. Several short sessions are better than one long one
- undertake revision and study in a regular convenient study area
- write notes, rewrite them, check your understanding of them

179

- practise writing to time
- use charts, sticky notes and drawings around your house to remind you of key aspects of your learning
- familiarize yourself with past papers – content, layout and answer conventions
- *The night before*: have a good night's sleep before an important examination. Look briefly at your final notes before sleep. Prepare your equipment and clothes ready for the next day. Set the alarm in good time.
- *Exam day*: have a good breakfast. Arrive in ample time allowing for transport delays. Avoid excited chat with other candidates – it will only worry you if they mention things they've revised and you haven't.
- *In the room*: read the whole paper carefully – rubric and questions – noting alternatives, ticking likely questions. Don't panic.
- *Timing*: the rubric tells you how many questions you should answer and how many marks there are for each question. Allowing ten minutes for reading the paper, organize a time budget so you know how long to spend on each question. Spend longer on questions giving many marks, and less time on questions giving fewer marks. Stick to your timing.
- *Selecting*: choose and mark the questions you are sure you can answer. Then mark the other questions you plan to answer.
- *Read through each question carefully before answering it*: don't jump to conclusions about what it means. Look for key words such as 'Discuss', 'Compare', 'Give your personal view' or 'Summarize the evidence for'.
- *Structure*: in essay-style answers, plan your answer with headings or key words in rough before starting to write. This will prompt you for what to write next and should stop you rambling off the point. A well-planned essay is easier to mark. Avoid a long preamble or introduction – marks are awarded for relevant points well made.
- *Write legibly*: don't imagine that an examiner will be fooled by your poor writing into thinking you can spell better!

Course work

Course work has gained a poor reputation in some quarters because it is difficult to identify how much is the pupil's own unaided work. This is rather unfair, as coursework aims rather to exemplify what a pupil can achieve with help from other pupils, external information sources and perhaps some family input. In that way it is more like a real-life collaborative piece of work than a solo examination.

A difficulty comes when pupils attempt to pass off some of the material as their own rather than acknowledging its source. Adapting material to make it your own by applying it to a new situation is an important study skill. Fortunately a combination of knowing your pupils' writing styles, being familiar with their drafts, and sometimes running questionable passages through a search engine can ensure that plagiarism is limited.

It is the working alongside pupils, making suggestions, offering comments and giving signposts, which are the great merits of coursework over examinations. As the work develops and takes new shapes, it becomes personal to the pupil, created by them with you, rather than an impersonal topic delivered by you because it's on an examination list.

Coursework allows the creative and self-motivated pupil to excel and be empowered, learning new skills and new knowledge in a quest for answers to their own personal project. It allows the diligent and the artistic pupil to shine by having a depth of research, a breadth of examples and a quality of presentation which does the content justice. And no, that's not advocacy of pretty covers over vacuous content, but enhancing already good content with hard work and appropriate design using wider learning skills.

An A-level course I taught had a coursework element valued at 33 per cent of the final total. It took a disproportionate amount of time in the second year of the course, but it was justified by the great and lasting learning opportunity to study the subject in a practical way. When a certain politician proclaimed the maximum value of marks could henceforth be only 25 per cent the balance was tipped and I opted for a timed examination instead. Result – loss of a rich learning opportunity.

Final products

Active learning requires that students actually do something with the product of their research or adapt and manipulate the information they have found. This will show whether they've really understood what they have been working on.

'Write a report on ...' is, however, not only dull, but also so vague that it doesn't test the child's ability to arrange their data. Worst of all is the instruction to 'Find out everything you can about ...' which is, almost by definition, a hopeless open-ended task and which offers no success criteria or useful framework in which to organize the information.

The following list contains suggestions which may be quirky and unusual, but could vary a monotonous diet of essays and report writing, should introduce variety into the range of written styles and organizational frameworks required, stretch most students and allow individuals' skills to shine. Some will be useful for displays, some for assessment, some for the sheer enjoyment of learning.

Art gallery
Creating a picture, perhaps a montage, of significant people, places and events, together with a 'catalogue' or commentary can encapsulate historical events, significant moments or important people.

Arts festival
An arts festival could be a final demonstration and culmination of lengthy rehearsals and training, or a way of bringing together a variety of responses to a similar topic. If pupils are given the choice of how they might present the results of their research and study, some might do so visually, others actively, according to their preferred learning styles. An arts festival (even a small class-sized one) can bring different groups together and provide a sense of audience.

Autobiography
Real or imagined (and an imaginary autobiography gives scope

for all sorts of creative invention), writing about yourself makes information personal and relevant. Relate a historical timeline to your family or emphasize local aspects of national events.

Banner
A simple and effective device to highlight important facts, key topics or opposing views in a debate; what does this person or topic represent?

Courtroom trial
A way of formalizing discussion into a debate. Who shall be pardoned and who punished in *Romeo and Juliet*? Was the USA guilty of war crimes by bombing Hiroshima? Non-participants can be reporters writing news briefings on the courtroom drama.

Debate
Another way of formalizing discussion. Planning speeches can be done individually or in groups, members of the audience can present brief points of view, and the whole debate, either summarized or videoed can be used again as a resource and as an assessment opportunity.

Book review
There is a risk that compulsory book reviews can put off readers and spoil enjoyment, but creating a class file of book reviews can help other readers searching for suitable reading and can help individuals form an opinion on what they have read. Entering reviews on a searchable database makes entry, retrieval and inclusion of pictures (thumbnail front covers from *Amazon* or general illustrations from *Google Image Search*) easy. Store the database in a central place for all classes to access it, or add it to the school website. When participants include their names they can simply search for their own entries (and so can you, for assessment purposes).

Brochure
This is an ideal format for highlighting the best 'selling points' of

a topic. A First World War battlefields tour, a local nature reserve, the school itself, are good topics.

Cartoon

Summarize a single idea, event or quotation; characterize people in stereotyped ways, or create a storyboard to tell the main events of a play, novel or a process. Remember that cartoons can be serious as well as funny!

Collage

Good for putting the emphasis on the idea and the message instead of artistic skills – though these can be incorporated too. Collected items such as dried flowers, tickets or newspaper cuttings are as valid as writing and drawing to record an atmosphere or an event.

Letters

Letters to those who helped make the trip possible or who contributed their materials or experience are valuable social lessons. Letters to real or invented people or to newspapers expressing views can help bring history to life. Letters as questions to experts (perhaps as an Ask An Expert online activity) focus on and can clarify important issues (how did you feel when you ... or why did you ...). The ability to write formal letters of complaint is a useful and important skill for all ages.

Machine

This need not be a functioning model (though that could be a great D&T project) but a drawing of a Heath Robinson device can show the water cycle, growth and decay, from raw material to processed goods or any kind of process – even the formation and construction of sentences.

Demonstration

As teachers know, demonstrating to the rest of the class is a highly effective way of showing whether we really understand our subject matter. Video it and we have an assessment opportunity too.

Diagram

A good diagram can express in a small space what would take many paragraphs to tell less clearly. It can also make concrete what might otherwise be abstract – one reason why mind maps are so helpful.

Diary

Personal reflection in a notebook, journal or diary is an important element in self-development. Used in class it's vital to set the ground rules first on who is entitled to read it and how it is to be used. Diaries have a right to stay private unless agreed otherwise.

Display case

Choose artefacts collected on a school trip, flowers and plants from a nature walk (rules and regulations apply), mementoes, etc., to make a display. A standard box size for each pupil is recommended. Non-valuable items.

Exhibition

At its simplest level this is 'show and tell'. However, it offers the opportunity to create a catalogue in which pupils explain their reasons and choices, and a visitors' book in which other pupils and visitors can record their impressions.

Experiment

Active learning involves pupils finding out for themselves rather than being given answers. That's what an experiment is too. It answers the question 'what happens when …' A successful experiment can be repeated to prove a case to a wider audience. There's no real reason why a safe experiment should not be performed by pupils for pupils.

Fact file

This is the simplest collection of materials – easy to collect but difficult to organize effectively. A teacher-provided framework in which the collection fits, and criteria for what can and what can't be included, is essential for a fact file to be effective.

Flag

This differs from a banner in that the symbol represents in graphic form the achievements or characteristics of a country or person.

Flip-chart

Good for organizing ideas logically. Think in terms of headings and subheadings. This method emphasizes the important elements and this can provide a framework which can later be turned into an essay or a presentation.

Flow chart

This emphasizes processes and links between ideas. The flow can be complex but a simple use of ideas linked by nodes where you answer yes or no can lead to effective decision-making. Very good for career choices and for simple adventure games. It's also possible to write a story of alternative narratives (should he: a) take the money, b) run away, c) jump over the cliff?). Board games can feature simple snakes and ladders-type events or more complex scenarios where taking a card from a pile requires you to answer questions or make decisions.

Activity games can be based around an orienteering course, where map-reading, decision-making and collaborative tasks are linked to physical activity – rather like a board game played in school grounds.

Heraldic shield

Similar to a flag, above.

Journal

Similar to a diary, but less personal. A journal can record events, as on a field trip or over a period of lessons marking the progress of an experiment. A teacher's professional journal is an important aspect of continuing professional development (CPD).

Lesson

Going beyond presentation, and with suitable aims, preparation and guidance, a group of children can present a lesson to the rest of the class. Learning is enhanced for the pupils who do the teaching, and the concentration and cooperation of the audience are often high. Any presentation by pupils gives the opportunity for assessment, but also the opportunity to learn more about the pupils themselves.

Magazine

Less news-focused than a newspaper, a magazine can be a great project for collaborative learning and teamwork. Colour illustrations, different text styles, layout and production all are excellent learning opportunities.

Model

A model shares some of the characteristics of a drawing and of a machine. Models of suitable 3D subjects such as battlefields, planets, dinosaurs, can give life and a sense of scale to many items.

Mural

A mural is a relatively permanent wall display. While a wall can feature art and written work, a mural could be a learning resource for a wider or longer-term audience. A mural by an art group in public spaces realizes a sense of audience. A mural can be a statement!

Museum

This is an extension of the display case idea. Can you convert an area of the school into a museum for a week? As the conclusion of a term's work on science or technology, this could be a museum designed to bring together more than one subject area which would appeal to and explain the subject to pupils from other groups.

Picture book

Rewriting or redesigning an existing book is both a language and a graphics project. Rewriting a classic story for a younger audience is an effective task involving an understanding of vocabulary, narrative and sentence structure, and the ability to rewrite for a different audience. When setting the criteria for the task, consider how the finished product can be printed or reproduced, so all members of the group can receive a copy.

Podcast
Similar to a radio programme this differs in the medium by which it is delivered – over an MP3 player rather than a traditional radio. The style is similar. Playback can be enhanced by adding still pictures and even hyperlinks.

Presentation
Presentation could cover either a straight talk from the front to the class or an all-dancing PowerPoint show. Presentation software can incorporate animated graphics, movies and sound, and can be kept as part of an electronic portfolio, while a spoken talk with more traditional visual aids demands more sense of audience, drama and nerves. Both require organization and an understanding of the topic.

Puppet show
It's remarkable how effective a puppet show can be. Just watching a small zone of action concentrates the mind of the audience, which soon accepts the conventions of the puppets. Hold puppet shows of scenes from plays and novels: costumes and scenery much cheaper than the real thing!

Scrapbook
Rather like a fact book, this collects together material without requiring much in the way of organization. A well-designed task would incorporate a framework where the pages of the scrapbook have clearly defined headings to help organize the material, or would use the scrapbook as a first stage towards a more complex task. Simply as a memento of a trip or visit, or the activities of a class over a year, it's worth keeping for its own sake.

Song or rap
With poetry still sometimes hampered by the question 'does it have to rhyme', a song or a rap provide different formats in which words take flight.

Time capsule

Deciding what should be kept and why makes this mainly a decision-making activity, but with the twist that the product of the exercise will remain. What would we like previous generations to have kept for us? What would we like to leave behind to represent us, our school, our civilization? If the time capsule is to be sent to another planet, what would we like them to know about us – and how are we going to explain the things, people and animals that we send?

Timeline

An essential in relating the chronology of history. Similarly valuable for any series of events – e.g. in geology, geography, history, fiction. A timeline around the classroom walls is a terrific visual aid and a good lesson starter.

TV or radio programme

Simple audio-visual equipment makes television-programme creation possible for a classroom teacher. The cassette recorder has been replaced by a laptop and integral microphone. Decide the responsibilities of the members of the production team (sound effects, technician, broadcaster, editor, etc.) and define the remit of the programme (documentary, vox pop, entertainment magazine, etc.) along with advice on how to achieve that style. Imitating the style of existing programmes is a useful flattery when it involves analysing the original.

TV or radio advertisement

Products, services and good causes can be advertised. Viewing and analysing a range of these in class will bring out the key features and how important points are put across in a very short time-frame. Try to avoid the oldest clichés which pupils will fall into, e.g. sounding like 1950s US broadcasters!

Verdict

This is a summary of the courtroom drama or the conclusion of a debate. It can force pupils to decide for themselves – preferably on evidence they've seen and heard.

Readability and suitability

For more on how to use ICT to produce effective learning materials you could go back to the pupil ICT skills referred to in Chapter 9.

Teacher-produced resources have the great benefits of being produced by the person immediately responsible for learning. However beautifully printed and thoughtfully created, a resource by someone else cannot match the immediate need in the same way as an inspirational idea by the class teacher.

Often an additional home-made sheet will clarify and refer to the professionally produced materials. This will emphasize what the teacher wants to be learned and at the same time demonstrate a degree of ownership by the teacher. This instruction or explanatory sheet need be no more than A4, black and white, prepared on a simple word processor. Sometimes a flip-chart or something drawn on a whiteboard will be just as good, with the advantage of immediacy and flexibility.

More elaborate presentations using presentation software, interactive whiteboards, Internet connectivity and movies are worthwhile if the topic is likely to recur with another group next year, or may be created as a collaborative resource to be shared with colleagues.

However, teachers do not, in the main, have sufficient time – and sometimes design skills – to produce all their own materials in the time available. Therefore some balance of teacher-produced and professionally published material is likely to be used. The teacher will mediate the material, explaining, translating, emphasizing and interpreting, and the class will have a fuller experience.

Buying suitable material even from acknowledged educational sources can be a problem, with publishers striving to aim for a wide multicultural readership by using examples and graphics that are politically correct and vocabulary and topics which are thought appropriate for the reader. However, what is appropriate for a private school in Berkshire may not grip the children of Belfast or Hackney; what is gritty realism for one may be feebly uninspired or irrelevant for another.

If you are fortunate enough to have a head of learning resources, you may be able to ask him or her for advice on suitable materials. They should have catalogues and connections to supply your need.

Readability is affected by both vocabulary and grammar. While it is a good thing to challenge a child's reading level with new words, this must be done in moderation if we are not to lose their interest when they fail to understand.

I used to start a talk to graduate teachers in training on the subject of 'Do our pupils understand us' with a couple of sentences in a lesser-known foreign language to illustrate how it feels to fail to understand what your teacher says to you. I followed this up with short (200-word) pieces of text from which

- 'difficult' words were replaced with blanks
- seven key words were replaced with nonsense words
- every eighth word was removed

These caused universal difficulty and helped us to imagine how difficult it is to understand what is spoken and written when even a small amount of data can't be understood. Pupils who have a small vocabulary or limited understanding – the very pupils who need help most – will be excluded and switched off. As we live our lives and process our learning through language, choosing appropriate readability, or mediating by explaining and inter-preting is a fundamental task for a teacher in any subject. Hence the much maligned phrase 'Every teacher is a teacher of English.'

Even when we talk to the class we must be aware of our language and its appropriateness. Long ago I noticed a pupil of mine had taken to writing the letters 'SA' on the top of her work, but they were not her initials. It turned out I had asked her to write an essay. As I had not written the word down she kindly added her neat label 'SA'. I also remember talking about the US state Pennsylvania, which one child wrote down as Pencil Vanier. I still have a delightful vision of slightly snooty pencils dancing in the woods.

Many pupils are not familiar with formal language register. Someone has to teach them the difference between the politeness terms 'could you', 'would you', 'will you' and the straight imperative. For them, 'Could you take this to Mr Setchell' may be a question, while for you it is a request. 'Will you stop that now' can be a question or a demand. 'Can I go to the toilet' can be a request or a query.

Some of these misunderstandings are only revealed in pupils' own writing, famously and apocryphally in examples such as:

What was myxomatosis? It was when they wiped out rabbis.

and in genuine examples from my own experience:

'I hate peas as I hate all Montagues and thee.'
'The Capulets were rude and the Montagues were well manured.'

and, from a story about a holiday:

'Mum and I were travailing in a mustard-coloured larder.'

Inaccuracy can reveal misunderstanding and it can also lead to it.

Vocabulary limitations can be caused by delays in learning to read, a poor home learning environment, dyslexia, and being given school materials which are at too high a reading level.

While a teacher may offer a topical lesson using a newspaper extract, the reading level may be too high. The teacher's own writing style may have too many passive sentence constructions or over-long sentences, all of which can hamper understanding.

It can be helpful to use the Microsoft Word built-in readability index. This gives the Flesch-Kincaid index which assigns an 'ease of reading' and US grade-school level score (1–12) based on the number words per sentence and number of syllables per word. Use on a variety of texts, including daily newspapers and your own writing, will help to match the readability level of a piece of writing to the reading age of your pupils. Microsoft Word suggests aiming for a score of approximately 7 or 8 for general documents, though a quick check on several British daily newspapers averages at 11–12.

Remember that about a quarter of the adult population have vocabulary levels of less than 12,000 words. Given their age, most of our pupils will be nearer the bottom end of this scale.

On a six-level scale vocabulary levels have been estimated as follow:

Level 1	0–6,000 words	Children 6–9 years old
Level 2	6–12,000 words	25 per cent of the adult population; children who will mature to Level 4
Level 3	12–18,000 words	Most common; 18 year olds in full-time education
Level 4	18–24,000 words	Majority of university graduates
Level 5	24–30,000 words	Top of professions; widely read
Level 6	30–36,000 words	Rare; people for whom this is an intellectual game

In a test of the 100 words from popular newspapers which, in the judgement of the researcher, came highest in vocabulary test levels, *The Times* had virtually all its words in Levels 4 and above, the *Daily Mail* in Levels 3 to 5 and the *Sun* entirely in Levels 3 and below. So the most widely read daily newspaper in the UK has no vocabulary more advanced than that of an average 18 year old.

In most subjects there is a core of essential vocabulary items. It is useful to create a wordbook for each department itemizing these key words and their meanings and providing explanations and examples of the words in use in daybooks and on classroom walls. The Special Needs department will find these helpful in checking the understanding of the less able.

The science department in my last school provided nearly 200 vocabulary items in 12 categories, all of which were considered essential to understanding science. That may seem excessive but it does no more than meet the requirements of the National Curriculum. Here are samples from each of the 12 categories. If you are a non-scientist you might reflect on whether you yourself can provide a definition for each word.

Investigating	Materials	Energy	Variety of Life
Observe	Classifying	Transferred	Photosynthesis
Measure	Properties	Joules	Chlorophyll
Kilogram (kg)	Natural	Potential	Arthropods
Hypothesis	Synthetic	Biomass	Chloroplasts
Forces	*Acids &* *Alkalis*	*Having* *babies*	*Magnetism &* *Electricity*
Friction	Alkaline	Testes	Poles
Resistance	Neutral	Cervix	Attract
Density	Distilled	Fertilization	Amps
Newtons	Pestle	Hormones	Current
Matter	*Environment*	*Rocks*	*Sight & Sound*
Expand	Habitat	Igneous	Image
Solution	Moulds	Sedimentary	Absorbed
Insoluble	Nutrient	Stalactite	Angle of incidence
Boil	Sterilized	Erosion	Ultrasound

You might also consider that words such as natural, transferred, poles, current and potential are ambiguous in that they have one general meaning in normal use and another specific meaning within science. I taught a group of Year 5 pupils fractions with little success until I realized they were working on the basis that a half was just two pieces instead of two pieces of identical size or weight. A group of Year 7s had great difficulty in realizing that the shadow of an object would always be on the opposite side to the sun (which made shadow clocks a bit confusing for a while).

The way words can be opaque while the sentence appears to make sense is clear in this example:

A thrim is a pook and it gribes mincingly.

1. What is a thrim?

2. What is a pook?
3. How do each of these gribe?
4. What on earth are you talking about?

It is of course possible to answer the first three questions entirely correctly without having a clue about the meaning of the sentence. We should avoid the possibility of this parrot response by clarifying the meaning of the words we use and setting questions which require thoughtful, personal, answers.

Factors affecting sentence complexity

Using the passive, negative or question forms.

a) Why are statistics about some kinds of crime not always reliable?
b) Statistics about crime may not be reliable. Why is this?

Prefer the active sentence with standard word order of subject, verb, object.

Elaboration
Groups of words which elaborate upon a single word.

a) The Princess picked a flower.
b) The Princess picked a beautiful pink flower from the gardener's favourite plot.

Keep it simple, don't over-describe.

Density
The amount of information in a sentence, its complexity.

a) If you were provided with three black-painted metal rods, one of which is made of brass, one of magnetized steel and another of unmagnetized steel, describe how, without scratching the black paint, you would identify each of the black rods.

b) Suppose you were provided with three black-painted metal rods. One is made of brass, one of magnetized steel and one of unmagnetized steel. Describe how you would find out what each rod is made of, without scratching the black paint.

Break a complex sentence into several shorter simple sentences.

Examination style is one area where teachers tend to revert to an old-fashioned and confusing formality. For example:

Multiple questions	'By finding ... and then looking at ... determine where ...'
Superfluous phrases	'Having read the extract above, you are now in a position to ...'
Metaphorical language	'The historical heartland of Scotland was eclipsed ...'
Distancing techniques (passive voice)	'It is generally considered that ...'
Hypothetical forms	'If the volume is four cubic centimetres, calculate the possible ...'

The 1988 Kingman Report on the teaching of English recommended considering:

Punctuation and its relationship with meaning
- the use of pronouns
- the structure of phases and sentences, including the choice of verb tenses
- word choice in relation to word meaning and appropriateness to context
- a knowledge of discourse types in writing
- a knowledge of language acquisition and development

An understanding of these features would certainly help a teacher to create resources and speak appropriately to facilitate learning.

Examples of resources for learning

Statements of theory about the benefits of methodical learning strategies are all very well, but practical lesson ideas and schemes of work are of most use to the classroom teacher and curriculum planner.

One-off events can create headline news, but subtle embedding in normal curriculum work can have a greater effect in the long term. It is only by embedding literacy, numeracy, citizenship, information literacy, ICT and other essential skills into our present subject-based secondary curriculum that we can ever hope to have these skills effectively learned. While the primary school classroom has a more flexible approach because, usually, a single teacher shapes the children's learning experiences, the secondary school has a much more rigid curriculum organization. Until the secondary curriculum breaks away from traditional monolithic subjects (as some 'alternative' schools have done) we can only hope for some cross-curricular activities, collapsed timetable events and infiltration of these essential skills into the current subject areas.

So how can we embed information literacy and study skills? First, we need to do a curriculum audit covering:

- The classroom
- Lesson plans and schemes
- In the curriculum
- In life – including parents at home, work experience, school visits, extra-curricular activities, etc.

The idea here is not to add extra work to the bulging curriculum but to find where these skills are already being taught (even if possibly under another name), as well as opportunities where these skills could fit in with minimum disruption.

There is no ideal curriculum because we all have different views about the amount of emphasis which needs to be placed on different topics and skills. Managers generally look for fairly fixed structures so they can assure themselves that this or that is being taught; teachers want both the security of knowing what should be taught (and the resources for teaching it) and the flexibility to go off spontaneously and follow class or personal interests. I've lost count of the number of times I've been told by my ex-pupils that they remember the times we went off at a tangent more than the times we strictly followed the syllabus! Is that National Curriculum heresy? I think it's good teaching!

Let's say we want to make sure that presentation skills are being methodically taught. We need to find a suitable place for these early in the pupils' time at the school where they can be taught specifically, then a couple of opportunities for them to be reinforced in other subject areas. We'd also like to build on this by having more advanced training in later years and more diverse opportunities to use the skills practically.

Say the curriculum audit shows four subject areas where presentation is already an important topic (perhaps art, D&T, English and ICT), so the art department decides to take this on and broaden its teaching to include some aspects of ICT, showing how presentation can be influenced by a variety of media. The ICT and D&T syllabuses are slightly modified to show that presentation may already been taught elsewhere and that they can build on prior knowledge when approaching the subject themselves. A similar process takes place later in the school, with the crucial factor being that a teacher of one discipline is assured that a teacher of another discipline is supporting them. Of course this is a simplification, as large secondary schools rarely teach the syllabus in the same sequence to all pupils, but the principle is there – teachers supporting teachers; the curriculum as a framework for skills as well as content; each area of the curriculum relating to the others to support coherent learning in a cooperative way. It is not, as they say, rocket science, yet in my experience it is rare to see such cooperation and mutual understanding in practice.

Mutual help on skills

Let me offer an example from my own school where each department helped the next by building on information skills.

Each of the following projects was an accepted part of the school year, modified and built on perhaps from year to year, but a gate through which every pupil had to pass.

English Year 7
A basic information skills programme using a library booklet and working in timetabled weekly slots in the resources centre. How to use the resources centre, how to find information and what to do with it when you've found it, culminating in an information treasure hunt. Every new Year 7 pupil visited the resources centre within the first two weeks of the new year, then one term emphasized non-fiction and information skills, another term fiction and reading.

Science Year 8
'The Planets' project was long established but, with the help of the librarian, new resources and computer terminals were provided, along with timetabled space. The head of resources helped produce a new lesson scheme and worksheets which featured information skills. Final presentations included model planets hanging from the resources centre ceiling.

Design & technology Year 8
An existing project on furniture was expanded to include some initial research using the 5/6-step plan to frame the process. The librarian bought specific resources to provide for the project on condition that pupils came to the resources centre to do their research.

History Year 9
A First World War topic was taught in advance of an annual field trip to the trenches. Some English teachers used this as an opportunity to look at First World War poetry and an English teacher was usually invited to the battlefields trip. The head of resources went along with some palmtop computers so pupils could record their experiences spontaneously. Photographs, pupils' trip diaries and materials collected from the trip were incorporated into a guidebook published on the school's website.

Geography and history Year 9

A local studies project was created to cover the areas where history and geography had gone their separate ways. The head of resources created a framework which incorporated existing aims and objectives for these two departments and added information and research skills. A 'virtual visit' of the nearby village was published on the school website along with census materials.

English Year 9

Disasters. This topic was chosen as an information skills activity because the topic was sufficiently wide-ranging and interesting for pupils, while generating varied output. It was also tied in to the skill of practical writing. Once again the information skills framework was used.

Embedding projects which use information skills into the curriculum so they are accepted and revisited by all teachers, ensures the idea will be integrated and that all the hard work involved in setting up the system once will not be lost in subsequent years. Ensuring each project is referred to in all relevant departments and school documents means it cannot be ignored.

Suggest cross-curricular projects

The examples of research projects above were similar in their use of information skills and mainly different in content. Here are some examples of topics which are similar in content and are relevant to more than one subject department. Although the list should be almost endless, in practice cross-curricular working in secondary schools is very limited.

Gatsby

An English teacher and a teacher of American history paired up and assigned research projects on the roaring 1920s and 1930s, in conjunction with the English class reading *The Great Gatsby*. At the conclusion they held a Gatsby Party, where the pupils arrived in the early evening dressed in roaring 1920s clothing, dancing to 1920s music, and eating food mentioned in the book. The research papers were assessed by the English teacher for English, and the history teacher checked their authenticity.

Insects

A science teacher looking at the life of insects paired up with an English teacher creating a poetry unit. Pupils wrote poems about insects. Mathematics followed up with a geometry unit, pupils drawing insects using a prescribed number of specific angles, shapes and line segments and looking closely at the bee dance which indicates to bees where the source of pollen may be found. In art the pupils made insects as hanging mobiles, while physical education/dance had pairs of pupils creating ways to move with 6 legs on the floor.

The First World War

In English pupils studied contemporary poetry and wrote news items, comparing actual items of news with news styles of today and contrasting soldiers' diaries with propaganda. In history the causes, events and politics of the period were examined and a joint trip to the battlefields culminated in a presentation to the whole year group and to parents, with pupil diaries and impressions published on the school website.

Developing the programme

Usually these joint projects start with two interested people coming together informally and roughing out a plan where they can see sharing and cooperating will be mutually beneficial. Maybe they have a common interest; perhaps they already share pupils. Their enthusiasm drives them on. The next step to two departments working together can be more of a problem and 'ownership' of the project is crucial. Each teacher and head of department must appreciate that the project is mutually beneficial, not just tagging along behind the other. It is not necessarily important that the two departments work together closely at first – that's a big bridge for some secondary teachers – but they should certainly have agreed to a joint plan.

The two original enthusiasts could here offer their time and experience and a head of resources, if you have one, and a librarian, can be invaluable in acquiring resources, creating timetable time in the resources centre, and any other facilities which will help the project become a success.

Planning a holiday

Web pages following this scheme are at
www.putlearningfirst.com/infohand/index

The basic idea is for pupils to 'Take the opportunity to plan the holiday of a lifetime with your friends! Imagine those happy days after your exams, lots of time to spend in the sun with your mates – but where will you go?'

There then follow a series of research tasks helping to produce the perfect summer holiday.

Lesson 1

1. Background to research. Six-Step Plan: Ask, Find, Do, Choose, Answer, Reflect.
2. Simple examples of planning before doing (organize a shopping trip, repair a bike puncture, etc.).
3. Emphasize reliability of evidence, the need for at least two sources where possible.

Task
'Plan a holiday for a group of your school friends in the weeks following your last examinations.' Some of this work could be done in groups.

Product
1. A letter to a newspaper requesting they suggest options for your trip: 'Please can you suggest a suitable place for us ...'

2. An informed newspaper article describing at least two suitable options in response to the letter request.

Lesson 2

Explain use of graphic organizers for collecting and organizing information.

Brainstorm all possible questions – who, why, what, where, when, how – and express them as questions to research answers.

Lessons 3–5

Produce a questionnaire to determine people's preferences for this kind of holiday.

Start researching holiday information on the web, using questions produced in the last lesson. Focus closely on the task. If working as part of a group collect all information in a single directory on the school network.

Starting points
1. Websites:
   www.travelocity.co.uk
   www.travelselect.com
   www.travelstore.com
   www.uTravel.co.uk
   www.easyjet.com
   www.go-fly.com
   www.ryanair.com
   www.guardianunlimited.co.uk/Archive (search for recent articles on holidays)
2. Use *World Travel Guide, Leisure & Tourism 338.4*, road atlases, other maps and atlases, travel guides especially *Eye Witness Guides* and *Rough Guides* 914, 917.47
3. Look in Saturday and Sunday holiday supplements.
4. Use Teletext if available.

Teaching points
Search, don't browse. Refer to the questions and the task. Look

for geographical information as well as holiday and leisure. Ask how reliable the source is – is it prejudiced? Does it offer a wide variety of holiday options?

Lesson 6–7

1. Re-emphasize task and product.
2. Recap Six-Step Plan – information skills, ask the question, brainstorm sources, search for answers.
3. Then select and choose suitable answers and begin to write up findings.
4. Write a letter to a newspaper stating your request and explaining what kind of holiday your group wants and doesn't want.
5. Select and choose from your previous research. Save into a directory of your own and start to layout and edit your newspaper article.

Deadline

By this time I need a printout of your newspaper article including:

- the letter of request
- at least two suitable options for holidays
- background details of accommodation, prices, dates, activities, etc.
- graphics of maps or photographs to illustrate the article
- reference to the questionnaire results showing young people's general holiday preferences

You should also be in a position to present this information to the rest of the class, if required.

Meat or veggie?

A Set of Internet research lessons supporting National Curriculum English.

Audience

Key Stage 3/4 English

Teaching objectives

- to practise information-handling skills
- to practise ICT editing skills
- to present an effective, informed and balanced argument

Timing

Five one-hour lessons plus extension tasks.

Reasons for using ICT

- availability of material with inherent bias from many sources
- material provided in digital form, so facilitating maximum editing and redrafting with minimum typing

National Curriculum references

English
- 'select, compare and synthesize information from different texts' En2 4a
- 'sift the relevant from the irrelevant and distinguish between fact and fiction, bias and objectivity' En2 4c
- 'to extract meaning beyond the literal . . .' En2 1a
- 'take different views into account' En1 3b
- 'sift, summarize and use the most important points' En1 3c
- 'plan, draft and redraft' En3 2a
- 'organize ideas and information, distinguishing between analysis and comment' En3 1n
- 'clarify and synthesize others' ideas' En1 3e
- 'use a range of techniques and different ways of organizing and structuring material to convey ideas, themes and characters' En3 1d
- 'distinguish features of presentation' En3 2c

- 'present material clearly, using appropriate layout, illustrations and organization' En3 1h
- 'analyse, review and comment' En3 7d
- 'use vocabulary, structures and grammar of spoken standard English fluently and accurately ...' En1 5 , En11f

ICT

- '[pupils] think about the quality and reliability of information, and access and combine increasing amounts of information.'
- how to collect, enter, analyse and evaluate quantitative and qualitative information ... KS3 1c
- designing information systems and evaluating and suggesting improvements to existing systems

Background information and notes

Security

These lessons require access to the Internet. The sites suggested are real world sites and, while they have been checked for suitability, no guarantee can be made that they do not link to other unchecked sites or that they have not changed since this lesson scheme was written.

Teachers are advised to check the sites in advance. Teachers with concerns are recommended to copy extracts from these sites and offer them as text files or place them on an intranet (copyright permitting).

Basic ICT skills needed

- use a browser to visit websites
- copy, paste and save web text materials into word-processed form
- edit, copy, paste, delete, insert text and save as a document

Preliminary issues

A preliminary discussion might take place before this lesson covering the following issues:

- the class's views on vegetarianism
- the ability to publish material on the WWW which is not subject to normal restrictions and can therefore be personal, defamatory, biased and untrue
- how we might evaluate the merits of a website

Evaluating material

Teachers are urged to read 'Evaluating information found on the Internet' by Elizabeth E. Kirk at www.milton.mse.jhu.edu/research/education/net. Kirk uses the following headings:

Authorship
Can you verify that the author knows what they are talking about? Is there a genuine contact address? Language errors may be a sign of a poorly educated author (pupils note!).

Publisher
Is the author from a recognized body or organization with a reputation and expertise? Has the work been published with their approval? Can you check the URL to see if the work is published personally or on the organization's official web space. What is the organization selling or pushing?

Point of view or bias
Is the author clearly pushing a single point of view or attempting to offer a balanced view? Is the page supported by a commercial organization with its own point of view? Kirk emphasizes: 'Never assume that extremist points of view are always easy to detect. Some sites promoting these views may look educational.' However, some obviously biased writers use intemperate language and offensive language is simultaneously an indicator that pupils should click away from a site that it is likely to offer an unbalanced view.

Referral to other sources

Does the author have a biography, bibliography, make reference to other work on the topic? Do they recognize that their subject is controversial?

Verifiability

Can the background information be verified for accuracy? Is there another source to confirm the views of this author? Are there criticisms or studies which put across another point of view?

Currency

When was the work published and when was it last updated? Is the data still relevant?

Further sites on evaluating sources and handling information

- Jamie McKenzie, *Creating Research Programmes for the Age of Information*, www.fno.org/oct97/question
- *Sheridan Libraries: Evaluating Information Found on the Internet*, www.library.jhu.edu/elp/useit/evaluate/index
- How to Evaluate a Web Page
  manta.library.colostate.edu/howto/evalweb
- Online! A reference guide to using Internet sources
  www.smpcollege.com/online-4styles~help
- Search *Google Directory* for 'information overload' or go to directory.google.com/Top/Reference/Knowledge_Management/Information_Overload/
- *How Much Information?* (2003) Research study at the University of California at Berkeley
  www.sims.berkeley.edu/research/projects/how-much-info-2003/

These sites could be the source material for a more complex measurement scheme for assessing the merits of websites.

Sequence of work

This will follow a planned approach to information handling, using the following stages:

Ask: ask the question, clarify the task
Find: the information sources
Choose: which are the most relevant information sources
Do: carry out the main task – identify evidence and arguments for both sides of the debate
Answer: write a discussion document using these points
Reflect: consider how successful you were in your task; consider how you might improve in future

Lessons

Five one-hour lessons plus extension tasks

1. Discuss
- the class's views on vegetarianism
- how the freedom of the WWW leads to published material which is not subject to normal restrictions and can therefore be personal, defamatory, biased and untrue
- how this makes it essential for users to be sceptical about what they read
- how we might evaluate the merits of a website

Commentary

You might collect the class's views and bring them out again after this series of lessons to see if ideas have changed following this exercise.

Compare the WWW with more traditional print media and consider who is responsible for book, film, radio and newspaper material.

What is the truth? How prejudiced are we all? Can we believe what a Spurs fan says about Arsenal and vice versa?

How do we evaluate the merits of books? What would you

look for in a book (author, date, design, suitability for age group, contents) – and what might you take for granted? (authoritative, accurate, edited, professional . . .)

2. Task
Present the task to pupils as follows:

> You are a pupil representative on the school council. You have been asked to do some research about vegetarianism because there have been arguments between some vegetarian pupils who refuse to eat in the school canteen while other pupils eat meat there.
>
> The situation is getting out of hand with groups of pupils holding extreme positions and you have been asked to present the facts in an unbiased way so there can be a calm and informed debate.

Method
Use the Internet. Visit the following websites:

- The Vegetarian Society of the United Kingdom
  www.vegsoc.org/
  www.vegsoc.org/youth/school/ks4/basics
- Why Vegan?
  www.veganoutreach.org/whyvegan/
- Are Humans Meant to Eat Meat?
  vegsource.com/joanne/qaphys
- Beef and Liberty!
  www.clues.abdn.ac.uk:8080/mirrors/growth/rep239nr
- People Eating Tasty Animals
  mtd.com/tasty/
- Why I eat Meat
  www.dgp.toronto.edu/~jade/thoughts/meat
- The Daily Nebraskan Opinion Story (meat eating is good)
  www.libfind.unl.edu/DailyNeb.arch/Fall97/Sept/091697/
  stories/091697/cullen
- British Meat
  www.meatmatters.com/index_flash

Evaluate each website using the checklist below. Distinguish between extreme views and apparent facts. Award points in a spreadsheet table as follows:

For each site give up to 3 marks for 'genuine, reliable, apparently unbiased, verifiable and up to date'. Give 0 marks for 'unreliable, no supporting authority, biased, no other sources mentioned, out of date'.

Feature	Site 1	Site 2	Site 3
Author			
Publishing body			
Biased/unbiased			
Other sources			
Verifiability			
Up-to-date			
Total			

3, 4. Process

Describe the Six-Point Plan as follows: Ask, Find, Choose, Do, Answer, Reflect. Explain how the process is important to make sure the task is carried out properly without jumping to conclusions.

If necessary give the example of planning a holiday:

Ask:	Do we want a holiday? Where do we want to go?
Find:	Information about all holidays – websites, printed brochures, people we know who have been, newspaper articles, library books, television programmes, our own recent experience ...
Choose:	Discuss and make our choice to narrow down our options to a reasonable number
Do:	Decide on details, consult with travel agent. Book it, confirm it.
Answer:	Go on it! Enjoy it!
Reflect:	Was it as good as you'd hoped? How could it have been better? What could you do to make it successful in the future?

Commentary
- Check pupils are selective in copy and pasting from the original to their own document.
- Pupils who have difficulty in selecting appropriately may first save a whole page of the original as a text document then delete unnecessary text until only the most important elements remain. This 'Trash and Treasure' method can be effective.

5. Product
The product should now be completed with a title, reasons for, reasons against and a conclusion written by the pupils and based on the evidence collected.

Extension tasks
1. Use the word-processed text and import into a desktop publishing package. Use graphics from the sites visited. Decide whether to produce an A5 pamphlet or a newspaper-style A4 sheet.
2. Use the word-processed text and import into a Web Editor. Use graphics from the sites visited and produce a web page for your school website.

Finally
- Present the case to the class or to other classes for debate.
- Compare with the findings from the original class discussion.

An all-purpose data capture tool

Use the sheet below and the empty boxes to guide pupils into asking pertinent questions and noting down appropriate answers. You will be able to see at a glance how fully they've completed the task and to 'offer appropriate encouragement'. The contents of the boxes can then be repurposed in another medium for final presentation.

An electronic version of this gives scope for different sizes of boxes.

Ask:

Make sure you know the task. What do you need to know?

```



```

Find:

Some sites have been found for you.

```
[examples in here]

```

Choose:

Last lesson you selected the most reliable sites. Write them here:

```



```

Visit the most reliable sites again.

Do:

Select and choose text carefully from these sources and save it.

```



```

Answer:

Compile a document containing the main arguments for and against the topic or the main issues influencing this topic.

```



```

Reflect:

Have you followed all the steps?

Have you collected enough information about the issue?

Have you organized your information into for, against and general?

How might you have done the task more effectively?

```



```

Appendix 1

MORI poll

Which three of the following do you do most often in class?

Students ...	2002	2000
Copy from the board or a book	67%	56%
Listen to the teacher talking for a long time	37%	37%
Have a class discussion	31%	37%
Spend time thinking quietly on their own	24%	22%
Work in small groups to solve a problem	22%	25%
Take notes while the teacher talks	20%	25%
Talk about their work with a teacher	16%	22%
Learn about things that relate to the real world	12%	11%
Work on a computer	10%	12%

These are the results from MORI survey commissioned by the Campaign for Learning of over 2,500 secondary pupils in 2002. Published in: www.campaign-for-learning.org.uk/pdf/policy/teach_pupils_learn.pdf

Appendix 2

WebQuests to try

From www.ictadvice.org.uk

- *Black and Asian soldiers in the First World War* WebQuest. The contribution of soldiers from the British Empire during the Great War.
- *Olaudah Equiano* WebQuest. Tasks on the Atlantic Slave Trade, through the eyes of Olaudah Equiano.
- *Black British History* WebQuest. An introduction to Black

British History through key individuals such as Mary Seacole and Olaudah Equiano.

- *European Dictators* WebQuest. Researching the dictatorships of Hitler, Mussolini and Stalin to compile a secret report on each leader.
- *Medieval Times* WebQuest. Life in the Middle Ages, from food to medicine, through the production of a play.

Also visit

www.webquestuk.org.uk
webquest.sdsu.edu
webquest.org
school.discovery.com/schrockguide/webquest/webquest

Bibliography

Belbin, R. Meredith (2003) *Management Teams – Why they succeed or fail*, 2nd edn. London: Butterworth Heinemann.

Berger, Pam (1998) Internet for Active Learners. Chicago, IL: American Library Association.

Bloom, B.S. (ed.) (1956) *Taxonomy of Educational Objectives: The classification of educational goals: Handbook I, Cognitive Domain.* New York/Toronto: Longmans, Green.

Boswell, James (1979) *The Life of Samuel Johnson*. London: Penguin.

Boxall, Marjorie (2003) *Nurture Groups in School: Principles and Practice*. London: Paul Chapman.

Butler, Kathleen A (1987) *Learning and Teaching Style: In Theory And Practice*. Columbia, CT : The Learner's Dimension.

Carter, Rita (1999) *Mapping the Mind*. University of California Press.

Carver, S.M., Lehrer, R., Connell, T. and Ericksen, J. (1992). 'Learning by hypermedia design: Issues of assessment and implementation', *Educational Psychologist* 27 (3): 385–404.

Children and their Primary Schools (The Plowden Report). London: HMSO 1967.

Cowley, Sue (2005) *Letting the Buggers be Creative*. London: Continuum.

Dale, Edgar (1969) 'Cone of experience' in *Audio–Visual Methods in Teaching. Visual Methods in Teaching*, 3rd edn. New York: Holt, Rinehart and Winston.

De Bono, Edward (1987) *Six Thinking Hats*. Harmondsworth: Penguin.

Dede, C. (1996) 'Emerging technologies and distributed learning', *American Journal of Distance Education* 10 (2): 4–36.

Department for Education and Skills (1999) *The School Curriculum and the National Curriculum: Values, Aims and Purposes*. London: DfES.

Eisenberg, Michael B. and Berkowitz, Robert E. (1990) Information Problem Solving: The Big Six Skills Approach to Library and Information Skills Instruction. Norwood, NJ: Ablex Publishing.

Feuerstein, R., Rand, Y., Hoffman, M. and Miller, R. (1980) *The Instrumental Enrichment*. Baltimore, MD: University Park Press.

Gardner, Howard (1983) *Frames of Mind*. New York: Basic Books.

Gardner, H. and Hatch, T. (1989) 'Multiple intelligences go to school: Educational implications of the theory of multiple intelligences', *Educational Researcher* 18 (8): 4–9.

Grey, Duncan (2005a) *ICT in English: Adding Challenge, Improving Engagement*. Bristol: Tribal Education/CTAD.

Grey, Duncan (2005b) *100 Essential Lists for Teachers*, 2nd edn. London: Continuum.

Hay, McBer Report (2000) *Research into Teacher Effectiveness*. London: DfES.

Herring, James (1999) *Teaching Information Skills*. London: School Library Association.

Higgins, S., Miller, J., Wall, K. and Packard, N. (2005) *Learning about Learning: Developing digital portfolios in primary schools*. Newcastle upon Tyne: Newcastle University.

Jacot de Boino, Adam (2005) *The Meaning of Tingo*. London: Penguin.

Jansen, Barbara A. (1996) 'Trash and treasure,' *School Library Media Activities Monthly*, February.

Kelly, G. A. (1955) *The Psychology of Personal Constructs*. New York: Norton.

Kingman Report (1988) *Report of the Committee of Inquiry into the Teaching of the English Language*. London: HMSO.

Kirriemuir, J. and McFarlane, Angela (2004) Literature review in *Games and Learning*. Nesta Futurelab.

Lazear, David (1991) *Seven Ways of Teaching: The artistry of teaching with multiple intelligences*. Palatine, IL: IRI Skylight Publishing.

Lazear, David (1992) *Teaching for Multiple Intelligences*. Bloomington, IN: Phi Delta Kappa Educational Foundation.

Leadbeater, Chalres (2003) 'Seeing the Light'. *RSA* [Royal Society for the Encouragement of Arts, Manufactures and Commerce] *Journal*, February 2003.

Leadbeater, Charles (2005) *The Shape of Things to Come – Personalised Learning Through Collaboration.* London: DfES Innovation Unit.

Learning Research and Development Center, University of Pittsburgh (1991) *The New Standards Project: An Overview.* Pittsburgh, Pl.

Lipman, Matthew (1985) 'Thinking skills fostered by philosophy for children' in Segal, J.W., Chipman, S.F. and Glaser, R. (ed.) *Thinking and Learning Skills,* Vol. 1. Hillsdale, NJ: Lawrence Erlbaum Associates, pp. 83–108.

Lipman, Matthew (1991) *Thinking in Education.* Cambridge: Cambridge University Press.

LISC Report (1985) *School Libraries: The Foundations of the Curriculum.* London: HMSO.

McCarthy, B. (1981) *4MAT system: Teaching to learning styles with right/left mode techniques.* Oak Brook, IL: Excel.

McGuinness, Carol ((1998) *From Thinking Skills to Thinking Classrooms.* London: DfEE.

Maccoby, E.E. and Jacklin, C.N., (1974) *The Psychology of Sex Differences.* Stanford, CA: Stanford University Press.

McKenzie, J., and Bryce Davis, Hilarie (1986) *Filling the Tool Box – Classroom Strategies to Engender Student Questioning* (online). www.fno.org/toolbox.html (accessed December 2005).

Miceli, Frank, 'Education and reality', reprinted in Postman, Neil and Weingartner, Charles (1971) *Teaching as a Subversive Activity.* Harmondsworth: Penguin.

Monty Python and the Holy Grail (1975). Directed by Terry Gilliam and Terry Jones.

Noble, Colin and Bradford, Wendy (2000) *Getting it Right for Boys – and Girls.* London, New York: Routledge.

Newton, Michael (2003) *Savage Girls and Wild Boys: A History of Feral Children;* London: Faber and Faber.

Ofsted (2003) *Boys Achievement in Secondary Schools* (HMI 1659). Also available from www.ofsted.gov.uk/publications/ (accessed December 2005).

Reynolds, D. and Muijs, Daniel (2001) *Effective Teaching*. London: Paul Chapman.

Rumsfeld, Donald (2002) Speech at a Defence Department Press Briefing, February 12th.

Rymer, Russ (1994) *Genie: A Scientific Tragedy*. London: Harper Perennial.

Seels, B. and Richey, R. (1994) *Instructional Technology: The Definition and Domains of the Field*. Washington DC: Association for Educational Communications and Technology.

Smith, Alistair (1996) *Accelerated Learning in the Classroom*. Stafford: Network Educational Press.

Stephenson, Susan (2000) *Child of the World: Essential Montessori for Ages 3–12+ (Michael Olaf's Essential Montessori)* (online), (16th edn) Michael Olaf Company. Available from: www.michaelolaf.net/ (accessed July 2005).

Stott, Philip. Letter to *The Times*, 22 June 2005.

Thomas, Gillian and Thompson, Guy (2004) *A Child's Place: Why Environment matters to children*. Green Alliance/Demos Report. London: Green Alliance/Demos, May.

Tiffin, John and Rajasingham, Lalita (1995) *In Search of the Virtual Class – Education in an Information Society*. London and New York: Routledge.

UNESCO/IFLA School Library Manifesto 2000. Found at: www.unesco.org/webworld/libraries/manifestos/school_manifesto.html

Winebrenner, Susan (1992) *Teaching Gifted Kids*. Minneapolis, MN: Free Spirit Publishing.

Work–Learning Research (2005) *Bogus Research Uncovered* (online). Somerville, MA. Available from www.work-learning.com/chigraph.htm (accessed December 2005).

Additional Online Sources

These are listed on a single page on the author's website at:

www.putlearningfirst.com/infolit/btlearn.html

Index